YOURS
FOR INDUSTRIAL
FREEDOM

YOURS FOR INDUSTRIAL FREEDOM

The Industrial Workers of the World from the Inside

ERIC THOMAS CHESTER

Levellers Press
AMHERST, MASSACHUSETTS

Copyright 2017 by Eric Thomas Chester

All rights reserved.

No part of this book may be reproduced or transmitted in any form or by any means electronic or mechanical including photocopying, reprinting, or on any information storage or retrieval system, without permission.

Cover image of the Bisbee Deportation courtesy
Arizona Historical Society, Library & Archives, #42669

Published by Levellers Press, Amherst, Massachusetts

Printed in the United States of America

ISBN: 978-1-945473-23-4

To the Next Generation of Wobblies

Table of Contents

Chapter One: *Introduction* — 1

Section One: Difficult Issues

Chapter Two: *The Centralization Issue* — 7
Chapter Three: *Sabotage* — 18
Chapter Four: *Violence* — 40

Section Two: Key Confrontations

Chapter Five: *The Bisbee Copper Strike, 1917* — 73
Chapter Six: *The Lumberjack Strike, 1917* — 100
Chapter Seven: *Frank Little* — 129

Section Three: World War I

Chapter Eight: *Opposing the War* — 153
Chapter Nine: *Conscription* — 171
Chapter Ten: *Confronting Repression* — 196
Chapter Eleven: *Conclusion* — 213
Suggested Readings — 215
Chronology — 217
Glossary — 224
Notes — 229
Index — 247
About the Author — 250

Acknowledgments

I would like to thank the many archivists who have helped me while I researched the history of the Industrial Workers of the World during the World War I era. I would particularly like to thank the archivists at the Special Collections section of the University of Warwick who went out of their way to acquire a complete set of microfilm of *Solidarity*, the IWW newspaper.

Many of the documents reprinted in this book come from the complete transcript of the Chicago conspiracy trial of 1918. The only extant copy of this transcript is found in the National Archives in College Park, Maryland. Undertaking research at the National Archives is a daunting prospect, but the archivists there went out of their way to help me.

My partner Susan Dorazio has assisted my efforts to complete my research on the IWW, an effort that has lasted many years. Her patience is appreciated.

Introduction

On September 5, 1917, agents from the Bureau of Investigation (renamed the Federal Bureau of Investigation or FBI in 1935) carried out raids on IWW halls around the country. A vast number of documents were hauled away during these first raids and many more were seized during the numerous raids that followed. This huge collection of documents was brought to the Chicago headquarters of the Bureau of Investigation, where a special team sorted through them to compile dossiers for use by government prosecutors.

Three weeks later, a federal grand jury in Chicago handed down 116 indictments of IWW leaders across the country. The resulting trial for conspiracy to obstruct the war effort and the draft in violation of the Espionage Act lasted for five months. Throughout the spring and summer of 1918, jurors listened to testimony from dozens of witnesses for both prosecution and defense. In the course of the trial, the prosecution introduced hundreds of documents chosen from the enormous trove of material seized during the raids. Most of these documents were letters exchanged between key IWW leaders, while among the other documents were internal bulletins, account books and poems.

Most of the defendants were found guilty and sentenced to long terms in a maximum security prison located in Leavenworth, Kansas. The IWW was determined to appeal the verdict through the appellate courts. Ultimately, both the U.S. Circuit Court of Appeals and the U.S. Supreme Court upheld the convictions and the IWW defendants were incarcerated for years before being released.

A prerequisite to the filing of the appeal was the preparation of a transcript of the entire proceedings. Only a few copies of the trial transcript have survived. Furthermore, the transcripts that have been available do not include the verbatim record of the documents introduced by the prosecution. The Bureau of Investigation prepared a dossier on each of the dozens of IWW leaders who were charged with violating the Espionage Act. (It is unclear whether the redaction of the trial transcript was prompted by a court order or a decision of the Department of Justice.)

For ninety years it appeared that all trace of this sizable collection of primary source material had disappeared. Indeed, Melvyn Dubofsky concluded in his standard work on the IWW that the documents seized in the raids on IWW halls had been "destroyed by federal authorities in 1923."[1] While researching a book on the IWW during the World War I era, I found in the National Archives in College Park, Maryland, a complete copy of the trial transcript, more than 15,000 pages in all, including the documents seized from IWW halls that were presented as evidence by the prosecution.

This anthology is primarily based on those documents. They present a picture of the IWW from the inside. I have supplemented this material with articles, poems, and cartoons drawn from the IWW's press, along with documents taken from the brief submitted by the defendants in their appeal of the verdict in the Chicago trial. The Wobblies created a lively sub-culture using songs, cartoons and short stories. These projected an image of the union as it wished to be seen. Although interesting, the images presented to the public by the IWW do not provide a complete, balanced picture of the union.

The correspondence drawn from the trial transcript shows the IWW grappling with many of the same problems that still confront the Left today. Indeed, the private letters of union leaders, and rank-and-file members, provide new insights into the IWW as it really was.

The legend of the Industrial Workers of the World has become an integral part of U.S. folklore. Wobblies liked to portray themselves as carefree, wandering troubadours. In reality, the situation was quite different. Most IWW activists were dedicated, committed radicals who concentrated their efforts on workplace organizing because they were convinced that a militant industrial union such as the IWW could become a critical component of a revolutionary movement that could effectively challenge the power of the corporate ruling class.

Documents drawn from the trial transcript show Wobbly activists debating a wide array of issues, ranging from the immediate tactics to be pursued to questions of fundamental strategy and theory. The IWW was far from monolithic. Indeed, there was a continuing and active interaction between the union's leaders and its rank and file.

The IWW that actually existed during its heyday was a much more interesting, and complex, organization than the romantic legend of popular folklore. The following documents provide us with a revealing glimpse into the union as it really was.

SECTION ONE : DIFFICULT ISSUES

The Centralization Issue

The IWW liked to project an image of itself as a loose band of wandering rebels, a union with no distinctly defined structure and in which everyone was a leader. This image remains an integral element of the romantic mythology that surrounds the IWW and yet it is contradicted by the actual functioning of the organization during its heyday. In reality, the IWW had a clearly defined structure, elected leadership bodies and a constitution that set the ground rules by which the organization operated.

The IWW placed a high priority on internal democracy and encouraged rank-and-file members to actively participate in the union. At the same time, Wobblies stressed the need for strong, militant industrial unions that could coordinate strike action that shut down entire industries. Furthermore, the IWW believed that an effective general strike would be the crucial tactic required to bring down the capitalist system. A general strike could only be organized by a structure that could act across industries in a coordinated fashion.

Given these conflicting priorities, the development of the union's structure led to a series of spirited debates. In 1913, IWW locals in the Pacific Northwest argued that the union was too centralized and that virtually all power should be devolved to the local level. This decentralization proposal would have sharply limited the power of affiliated industrial unions and would have stripped the general union of any authority.

Although those advocating decentralization represented a minority position, the union's leadership took the opposition seriously and influential leaders such as Vincent St. John and Big Bill Haywood fought to retain a more centralized model. They were convinced that the union would only be able to challenge the might of the huge corporations if the general organization continued to determine basic policies, and industrial unions retained the ability to coordinate direct action within their sector of the economy.

The fear that the Chicago headquarters was gaining too much power sparked an intense debate. Still, once World War I began in August 1914, most Wobblies understood the necessity for a coordination that went beyond the local level. Indeed, in spite of previous disagreements, the IWW functioned well during the crucial period following the decision of the United States to enter the war in April 1917. The union grew rapidly, while organizing effective, militant strikes in key industries such as copper mining and timber. During this period, the spring and summer of 1917, the existing structure of the union generally worked smoothly. The General Executive Board formulated the overall policy guidelines, in particular the attitude the union would take toward the war effort and conscription. Affiliated industrial unions determined the demands set by workers in that industry and made sure a strike that started in one locality spread throughout the industry. Locals, industrial union branches, determined the specific strategy to be used to organize workers in that area and the tactics to be used in implementing a strike once it was called. In general, the parameters of authority for each level were understood, and accepted, by most IWW activists.

Of course, problems arose as circumstances changed dramatically during a volatile period. The leaders of the Metal Mine Workers Industrial Union #800 engaged in a heated disagreement with the Bisbee branch concerning the demand for a six-hour day. When the leadership of the Agricultural Workers' Industrial Union #400 agreed to a tentative agreement with the Nonpartisan League, the authority of the General Executive Board to overrule the decisions of an affiliated union was brought into question.

The relative power of local and federated organizations in relation to the central headquarters and executive committee has consistently been a point of tension within organizations, and the IWW was no exception. The issue is discussed on both theoretical and specific levels in the following documents.

The first set of documents concerns the 1913 controversy. Vincent St. John, who was at the center of this debate, began working as a miner at the age of seventeen. In 1897, he moved to Telluride, Colorado, where he became president of the Western Federation of Miners local in 1900. He then led a militant strike the following year.

St. John joined the IWW at its founding in 1905 and served as its general secretary-treasurer from 1908 through 1914. In this position, he held the union together during a difficult period of slow growth. St. John was a thoughtful radical, who avoided bravado and boasting. He was greatly respected by the Wobbly rank and file, who nicknamed him "Saint." Shortly after the debate on centralization, St. John decided to not run for reelection at the September 1914 convention, and then, in January 1915, he left the IWW to become a prospector in New Mexico.[1]

St. John's belief that there was a role for a central coordination of the union's affairs brought him into conflict with locals in the Pacific Northwest. This encouraged him to formulate his views on the general issue of centralization. The following document provides his instructions to James P. Thompson, one of the IWW's most well-known speakers and a national organizer for the union. Thompson was sent to the 1913 convention of the Shingle Weavers' Union, an affiliate of the American Federation of Labor, in an effort to convince them to join the IWW. The convention voted to change the name of the union to the International Union of Shingle Weavers, Sawmill Workers and Woodsmen. This name change indicated an intention to become an industrial union covering all workers in the timber industry, including the lumberjacks, rather than a craft union restricted to a specific category of skilled workers, the shingle weavers. Thus, the approach to the timber union to affiliate with the IWW. In the end, the IWW's effort failed, as the renamed union remained within the AFL. In 1915, it dropped its effort to widen its jurisdiction, and again became the International Union of Shingle Weavers.[2] The IWW would charter an affiliate in early 1917 that would organize lumberjacks into a militant, radical union, with AFL affiliates remaining an insignificant factor in the lumber camps of the Pacific Northwest.

DOCUMENT ONE

Letter
Vincent St. John to James P. Thompson

Mr. J.P. Thompson
Raymond, Washington

Fellow Worker:

Find enclosed, herewith, credentials from the general organization for use at the Shingle Weavers' Convention. I am also enclosing [for] you herewith a copy of the constitution of the I.W.W., which you can use in showing up the report of Folsom of the Shingle Weavers, wherein he uses Moyer's letter, and attempts to make it appear as if the membership of the I.W.W. were allowed to have a voice in the legislations adopted by the conventions prior to the Second Convention. You will see by this constitution that there is no referendum provided so far as the actions of the convention are concerned.[3]

You are well acquainted with the history of the Second Convention to be able to handle the rest of the report of Folsom. You can also make it plain to them that, in case of affiliation with the I.W.W., what would be done is to call a convention of all the lumber workers organized in the I.W.W. and organize a National Industrial Union of Lumber Workers, and that the National Union would manage its own affairs, the same as the Textile Workers. I am enclosing you herewith a copy of the Textile Workers Constitution.

Whatever tax is paid into the general organization by the Shingle Weavers, arrangements can be made so that all of it is expended in organization work in that industry. In other words, the general office will pay the expenses for an organizer or organizers out of the tax received, and the lumber workers can designate the organizer, as long as he is a good revolutionist, and in accord with the principles and program of the I.W.W.[4]

Folsom tries to give the impression that in case they become part of the I.W.W. they will be ruled from the top.[5]

This point is one that you want to clear up for him, and show how local unions have the fullest and freest control of the local affairs; national unions and departments [have] the same control over the affairs of the industry or department, and it is only where the interests of the whole organization are involved that the general organization exercises any power whatever.

>Wishing you success, I am with best wishes
>Yours for Industrial Freedom,
>Vincent St. John
>Gen. Sec'y

P.S.: You can quote Haywood as in favor of the "Weavers" coming in the I.W.W.

Think Bill will be on the road for us before long.[6]

Make them come in the open.

The only membership we claim is 6180 paid up.[7] 400 out of work stamps.

IWW Transcript, pp. 10731-2

Shortly after his letter to Thompson, IWW leaders came to suspect that locals in the Pacific Northwest were preparing to quit the union, and were using the demand for local autonomy as a rationale for this split. St. John was convinced that the Portland, Oregon, local was the focal point of the effort to split the union. His response was to try to secretly organize a concerted effort to flood the Portland local with members committed to a unified organization.

This was a highly dubious action, particularly given St. John's earlier argument for a union structure that retained a great deal of local autonomy. There is no evidence in the records that St. John's strategy to flood the Portland local was ever implemented.

DOCUMENT TWO

Letter
Vincent St. John to Jack Law

August 29th 1914

Mr. J.A. Law
General Delivery
Sweetgrass, Montana

Fellow Worker:

Yours of the 4th inst, at hand and glad to hear from you. With reference to your request for back copies of the paper, will state that there are none in the office at this time. Will make an effort to dig up some, and, in case I do, will send them along. Am afraid, however, that you will be on your way before papers would reach you.

Note how you are situated; also your suggestion re unemployed in large cities. In this matter, will state that under present conditions the unemployed agitation in large cities would be a tough proposition. The police are right on the job, and have their stool pigeons on the watch for any indications along the line of organization. Because of this fact, they are able to swing whatever force is necessary to break up proposition before it gets well started. This, of course, means that the only result of any agitation that might be started would be to victimize the few who could take an active part in getting things going.

With reference to your being ready to take up any proposition and promise to get results, I have a suggestion to make. It appears at this time that the last stand of freak elements is going to be made in Portland, Oregon. They have moved the *Voice of the People* to Portland, and Hall has also located in that section. From letters that are sent to me it appears that what is left of the outfit are going to make a last effort to keep the Voice of the People in the field by changing the name to the *Industrial Worker*, and thus carry on the dissensions with the hope of splitting off the northwestern section from the General Organization.[8]

If you can arrange to get a good sized bunch of the right fellows together, and make Portland some time in the near future, colonize the local and take charge of the entire proposition, I believe the effort would result in direct benefit to the I.W.W.

Any move that would be made along this line would have to be made with caution, and you would have to exercise care in picking out men to drop into Portland. The idea would be to have fellow workers who are not well known to make the local first. Otherwise, the outfit there might get wise, and I have no doubt that if they did they would call the police to help them out.

Study this matter over and see what you think you can do, and let me know. Conditions in the organization are about the same as usual. Very little friction, if any, and, as stated above, the Portland outfit is the only bunch left that is attempting to cause any dissension. Conditions, of course, are a long ways from what they ought to be, and the war is making matters worse.

With best wishes, and hoping to hear from you in the near future, I am

  Yours for Industrial Freedom,
  Gen'l Sec'y Treas

IWW Transcript, pp. 12174-6

Although the divisive debates of 1913 were never formally resolved, the union remained together and the local organizations of the Pacific Northwest were instrumental in organizing the strike of lumberjacks in 1917. Relations between the Chicago headquarters of the IWW and the central office of the Lumber Workers' Industrial Union #500 in Spokane were harmonious throughout the spring and summer of 1917.

The same could not be said of the relations between Chicago and the headquarters of the Agricultural Workers' Industrial Union #400 in Minneapolis. The AWIU was seen by IWW activists as the most moderate element within the union, the section most concerned with creating a union that could negotiate specific concessions from employers. In the summer of 1917, the AWIU negotiated a formal contract with farmers in North Dakota.

Populist sentiment was very strong in North Dakota, leading to the formation of the Nonpartisan League, which presented candidates for state office who campaigned on the NPL platform within the two party system. The NPL rapidly spread throughout the state, becoming so influential that in 1916 it elected the governor and a majority of one house of the legislature on a program of social reforms. Thus, it made sense for the Nonpartisan League to represent its farmer-members in negotiating a contract with the IWW covering migrant workers hired during the harvest season.

The IWW generally avoided signing contracts, particularly written ones, holding that formal contracts limited the ability of the workforce to join solidarity strikes, or to strike the employer for improvements in wages and working conditions should the situation change in favor of the workers. On its surface, the tentative agreement specifically allowed either side to terminate the contract at any time. Nevertheless, it is clear that the agreement was intended to bind both sides for the length of the 1917 harvest season.

More importantly, the agreement explicitly holds that the farmers and the migrant workers they hire share a common goal that will be advanced through collective bargaining. This goes directly contrary to the essential premise of the IWW as stated in the Preamble of the 1905 Constitution, that is that employers and workers have fundamentally conflicting interests. The situation in North Dakota was more complex than this. Farmers were being squeezed hard by the banks and the railroads. These were not large capitalist enterprises, but small, precarious ventures. Nevertheless, the objective situation pitted farmer against farm worker.

It is, therefore, understandable that the General Executive Board insisted that the members of the AWIU ratify the contract by referendum vote before it could be implemented. As it happened, the president of the Nonpartisan League, Arthur Townley, rejected the tentative agreement after receiving pressure from some NPL members who believed that the contract established a wage rate that was too generous. Still, in much of North Dakota farmers hired IWW migrant workers during the 1917 harvest and paid them in accordance with the tentative agreement.

DOCUMENT THREE

Tentative Collective Bargaining Agreement

PROPOSED TENTATIVE AGREEMENT BETWEEN THE NATIONAL NONPARTISAN LEAGUE OF NORTH DAKOTA AND THE AGRICULTURAL WORKERS' INDUSTRIAL UNION OF THE I.W.W. FOR THE HARVEST AND THRESHING SEASON OF 1917

[July 1917]

WAGES

For harvesting, the wage shall be $4.00 for 10 hr. day. Overtime 40c per hr.

For threshing, minimum wage $4.00 for a 10 hr. day.

Should wheat sell at $1.75 per bus. Wages to be $4.50
Should "   " " $2.00 "   "   "   " " $5.00
Should "   " " $2.25 "   "   "   " " $5.50
Should "   " " $2.50 "   "   "   " " $6.00

10 hrs to constitute a day's work, and overtime to be paid on all threshing work at the proportionate rate per hr.

COMPUTATION OF TIME

Harvesting: The 10 hr. schedule for harvest work means 10 hrs in the field. Drivers of horses to care for them on their own time. Harvest workers not driving teams to aid in the odd jobs and chores without charge for overtime, but not exceeding time equal to that required in caring for a team.

Threshing:[9] Teamsters to care for their teams without charge for overtime. Time to run from the time the machine starts until it stops. Temporary stops of the machine during working hours, not exceeding 15 minutes at one time, shall not be deducted from the worker's time. Stops exceeding 15 minutes to be deducted at the full time of stop. No reductions in the time of the worker to be allowed for moves requiring less than 1 hr. for the move. On moves requiring more than 1 hr. the time to be deducted.

PAYMENT

Payment of wages to be cash on being discharged or quitting the job.

WORKING CONDITIONS

In all cases, food supplied to workers is to be wholesome and plentiful. The sleeping accommodations to be the best possible under the circumstances surrounding the job. Good faith to be exercised in the furnishing of these accommodations to the best of the ability of the employer.[10] In threshing, when laid up because of wind, rain, or other unavoidable casualty, free board shall be furnished by the employer for the first 3 days of each delay. After the first 3 days, the workers shall pay board at the rate of $1.00 per day. It is understood that the Agricultural Workers' Industrial Union is opposed to gambling and drinking amongst its members, and will use its best efforts to prevent it.

The Conditions of Employment

The right to discharge and the right to quit are understood and agreed to. Complaints concerning the violation or abuse of the specifications contained herein, by either employer or worker, shall be made by the individual to his own organization, through the proper delegate, or committee appointed for that purpose; each organization to hold its members responsible to it alone, and both employers and workers to be subject to the discipline of their own organization alone.

The members of the League are to employ only members of the A.W.I.U. provided sufficient help is furnished by it, except that men working by the season or by the month, or living permanently in the community, may be employed by the members of the League. The members of the A.W.I.U. to accept employment by none but League members until sufficient help has been furnished to them. The League is to use its best efforts to secure free transportation to all workers needed for members of the A.W.I.U. over all railways entering N. Dak. from the industrial centers.

Either organization may cease operations under this agreement at any time, on notice to the other. Should any portion of the State of North Dakota refuse to ratify this proposition, it shall operate only in those portions in which it is ratified by the League members. The League will use its best efforts to have it ratified by the membership of the entire state. It is understood that this proposition is nothing [other] than an honest effort of the League and the A.W.I.U. to cooperate to their mutual advantage. Therefore, both organizations pledge their most hearty and earnest effort to have the membership of each live up to cooperate in carrying out in good faith and fairness each and every specification contained herein, in a spirit of cooperation and good will.

IWW Transcript, pp. 11188-11191

Sabotage

Although the IWW rejected the use of violence directed at individuals, it proudly boasted of its willingness to employ sabotage. Still, the range of actions covered by this term was generally left vaguely defined. Sabotage could cover job actions in which workers slowed production by strictly adhering to rules that were normally ignored. Such a tactic could only be successful when the great majority of the workforce participated and could thus be viewed as a form of mass action. A variety of guerrilla actions could also be termed sabotage. For instance, workers could inform customers of the poor quality of the products being produced or sold. This type of action remained within the law, but it was not likely to be effective in bringing pressure on the employer.

Sabotage could also refer to acts of violence aimed at damaging property, a category covering a wide spectrum of actions. At one pole were acts of vandalism causing minimal damage. A worker could jam a machine or cut wood to the wrong specifications, while those on strike could damage the property of a strikebreaker. Often, the Wobblies who talked about setting the 'Sab Cat' loose were tacitly calling for this type of action. Sabotage along these lines involved little risk, but such actions were usually treated as a minor nuisance by employers, who did not regard them as a serious threat.

To the tabloids and government prosecutors, sabotage meant the use of force with the aim of causing substantial property damage. This could only occur through planting explosive bombs or setting fires. Sabotage on this scale leads to the same problems as those created by the use of violence against individuals, since bombs and fires frequently injure and kill innocent people.

There is no evidence that the IWW ever engaged in sabotage in this sense. The federal government tried hard to uncover evidence that the IWW had caused serious property damage and came up with nothing. On the other hand, unions affiliated with the American Federation of Labor sometimes used force to win a strike or organize the unorganized. The most notorious case involved the McNamara brothers, officials of the Bridge and Structural Iron Workers' Union, who dynamited a number of construction sites before an explosion at the *Los Angeles Times* building in October 1910 led to the death of twenty-one people.

When the United States declared war on Germany in April 1917, and the federal government began targeting the IWW for repression, the union reassessed its position on sabotage. In part, the decision to repudiate sabotage as a tactic was prompted by the illusory hope that this would enable the IWW to deflect government repression. At the same time, the successful strikes in Arizona's copper industry and the timber industry of the Pacific Northwest, in which the IWW explicitly avoided violence and relied on mass action, provided a further impetus to review the entire issue. Since 1917, the IWW has consistently rejected the use of violence of any sort, while calling for the building of a mass movement based on the working class as an alternative strategy.

Sabotage as Strategy

In 1912, the issue of sabotage became a subject of a bitter, divisive debate within the Socialist Party, as the Party's moderates baited a radical tendency linked to the IWW. The IWW responded by emphasizing its belief in the utility of sabotage as a tactic in the class struggle. Grover Perry, an influential Wobbly who would later become secretary of the Metal Mine Workers' Industrial Union #800, wrote the following signed editorial in an effort to clarify the union's position. Although Perry emphasizes the aspects of sabotage that avoid violence and that focus on restricting output, his last comments uphold the argument that any tactic that works can be adopted, a position that could lead to a willingness to destroy property and, perhaps, even to acts of violence directed at individuals.

DOCUMENT ONE

Editorial

Solidarity

February 1, 1913

Sabotage is a weapon that the capitalist class has used on the working class throughout the ages, a weapon that so-called revolutionary politicians have used, and are using, against militant working class throughout its history, a weapon that will be used in the future consciously by an organized working class with telling effect.

Reformers tell us that sabotage means death, destruction and violence. Preachers tell us it is unchristian. Nevertheless, it is being practiced by workers everywhere whether they realize it or not. Now, what does it mean?

Sabotage as practiced by craft unions, unorganized individuals and others, unconsciously and without clearly defined purpose, may mean all of the above things. Practiced by an intelligent working class, knowing why they practice it, and having a common goal to accomplish, it means none of the above.

Any action while on the job that will tend to be of benefit to the working class, or opposed to the interest of the capitalist class, can be construed as sabotage. Withholding of your efficiency as a worker is sabotage. Willfully curtailing production is sabotage. Forgetting to safeguard your master's interests, for example forgetting to lock up the premises, forgetting to turn off unnecessary electric lights, etc., is sabotage. Acts of sabotage are committed in every industry, and only need concerted action and a common goal to make them the most effective war measures in the fight between the master class and the working class.

You practice sabotage when you tell your prospective employer that you are a good worker when, perhaps, you are an indifferent one. You practice sabotage all the time; why not do it to some effective end. Nothing will bring a reluctant or obstinate employer to terms quicker than the knowledge that his entire workforce is practicing sabotage.

It doesn't matter what you work at, where there's a will, there's a way.

Cooks practice sabotage when they neglect to season food. Waiters practice sabotage when they delay serving food. Dishwashers practice sabotage when they neglect to rinse soap from dishes. Clerks practice sabotage when they give customers more than they pay for. Printers practice sabotage when they misspell words or pi type. Lumberjacks practice sabotage when they fail to saw logs clear through. Weavers practice sabotage when they make rag instead of fine fabric. You practice sabotage if you read this on the boss' time, and I practice sabotage if I get you to do it.

Everybody's doing it. Let's do it together. The ethical side of it need not concern us, as right and wrong are relative terms and do not concern the working class anyway. What's bad for the boss is good for us, always. What is good for the boss is always wrong for us as workers. Get the cobwebs out of your thinking machine.

Join the union of your class, and, if sabotage is practical, let the boss do the moralizing and worrying.

The following interchange examines the more positive aspects of sabotage as a tactic. Walter Hutchins was a skilled worker on the railroads and an active member of the Socialist Party. He was also a supporter of industrial unionism, a rarity among skilled railroad workers, who were organized into separate, independent craft unions, the railroad brotherhoods.

Hutchins' description of the use of a concerted slowdown as a tactic to be used by militant workers is an interesting one. Haywood's response pointed out that such a tactic depended on the mass support of the workforce involved, and thus provided the basis for more militant actions in the future.

DOCUMENT TWO

Letter

Walter S. Hutchins to William Haywood

Greenfield, Mass. July 14, 1915

Wm. D. Haywood
Chicago, Ill.

Fellow Worker:

In this part of the country, the railroad workers have repeatedly applied the principles of "sabotage," and, for the time being, with telling effect. To work it with success requires a solidarity which is seldom in evidence, but on several occasions it has been put into use, and, for a time, things were in an interesting setting.

The most effective application of this came in the winter of 1912. A new efficiency man was put into the position of traffic manager. At once, he proposed to run every train crew without a destination, but to continue on the road as near 16 hours as possible, then tie up for rest. Another crew was sent at once to continue on with the train. The crew first on the train, after taking rest, was to be sent to the nearest point, where another train was taking rest, to continue with that train. Sometimes it would be two weeks from the time a crew left home before it would return to the same point for rest.

At first, the men argued with him as to the right and wrong of such actions, as they could not get home regularly. And were informed in every case that "a home is a thing of the past on this road. Forget it." Then something happened. Knowing that they were in for a turn of 16 hours anyway, every rule was put into use, every means devised to make for the slowest time possible. And the result was that most of the trains had not covered enough ground in 16 hours but a passenger train could get them home in one hour or less. One train took the banner by covering the distance of 14 miles in 16 hours. With that as a record, everybody in the freight service tried in vain to beat it. But many were the crews that succeeded in covering less than 30 miles.

The result was that in six weeks the runs were put back on the former basis, with yards congested with traffic, but without a traffic manager. Runs were shortened and covered territory daily. The engines appeared to steam more freely, and, in time, the yard was cleared. But the boys did stick together splendidly. A hustler lost caste in a minute, and went lower scale among his fellows than a Russian muzhik in the eye of the Czar.[1]

This has also been used repeatedly when a road endeavored to burn some grade of coal such as is generally called "Director Coal." Several times has the road been literally tied up with traffic, [and brought] almost to a standstill. In every case, the men were informed that it was really Pocahantas coal, but workers as promptly named it "Hunt your poker coal," and traffic could not be handled by the director who owned the mine. So, something had to be furnished for fuel that would burn without too much work on the part of the tallow pot.

       Yours for Industrial Freedom,
       Walter S. Hutchins

IWW Trial Transcript, pp. 17091-3

DOCUMENT THREE
Letter
William Haywood to Walter Hutchins

July 17, 1915

Walter S. Hutchins
87 Conway St.
Greenfield, Mass.

Fellow Worker:

Have received your very interesting letter of the 14th, which clearly demonstrates that there can be such a thing as counter efficiency on the railroads, as well as other divisions of industry.

I note the change that has taken place since 1912, and the ingenious method adopted by the railroads at the instigation of the Interstate Commerce Commission. But I believe there are just as fertile brains among the workers, and, if they can be made to understand and practice solidarity, the situation would be in our hands so far as the railway service is concerned. Transportation is practically the keystone of the commercial life of this nation.

Your material can be used to good advantage. I am expecting a good meeting a week from Sunday of the Railway Workers Propaganda League. Think that some literature will be issued soon after that will in every way cover the railroad workers' situation, as well as the one you have issued, with perhaps something more definite in the way of propaganda. It will include an appeal to all railway workers, as well as the organized departments.

> With Very Best Wishes, I am
> Yours for Industrial Freedom,
> Gen. Sec'y-Treas.

IWW Trial Transcript, pp. 17093-4

Confrontation at Wheatland

The Durst brothers hop farm was one of the largest agricultural businesses in California, encompassing an extensive area near the small town of Wheatland, a few miles from Sacramento. In August 1913, the Dursts advertised widely for migrant workers to harvest the hop crop. Thousands arrived to find a tent camp with a few filthy outhouses and no nearby source of drinking water. Once the harvest began, the workers toiled twelve hours a day under the scorching sun. The pay scale was pitiful, and the system used to determine each pay packet further cheated the workers.

This volatile situation quickly exploded, as workers spontaneously organized and went on strike. A few IWW members were, by chance, among those who had come to Wheatland looking for work. Richard

(Blackie) Ford had been an IWW militant, but he was not a member in good standing at the time of the incident. Ford was an inspired organizer and speaker and he soon became the spokesperson for the strikers. Several other workers advised Ford, including Herman Suhr, a quiet Wobbly who acted as an intermediary between the strikers and the IWW.

Events moved rapidly in Wheatland, far too quickly for the IWW to effectively intervene. On August 3, 1913, several thousand strikers attended a mass rally demanding better working conditions, adequate sanitation facilities and higher pay. The sheriff of Yuba County stormed into the rally along with several deputies and the local district attorney, intending to arrest Ford for trespassing. This tense standoff sparked a gun fight, leaving the district attorney and three others dead, and the sheriff and one other person severely injured.

The confrontation at Wheatland was one of the crucial turning points in IWW history. In January 1914, Ford and Suhr were tried in a hostile environment, convicted of murder and sentenced to life imprisonment. The IWW was determined to free them, an effort that would become an acid test for the advocates of sabotage. Wobbly activists believed that if the rich and powerful could be convinced that keeping Ford and Suhr in prison would prove to be extremely costly, the authorities would be compelled to release them from jail. This strategy pushed the IWW down a questionable path, one that failed to deliver Ford and Suhr from prison, while at the same time leaving the union in a vulnerable position.

A February 1914 editorial in *Solidarity* presented the rationale for this strategy, which would then be put into practice over the next eighteen months.

DOCUMENT FOUR

Editorial

Solidarity

February 14, 1914

ANOTHER JUDICIAL CRIME

Herman Suhr and Richard Ford, Wheatland hop strikers, have been sentenced to life imprisonment in the California penitentiary at Folsom. The "argument" leading to their conviction by an evidently hostile jury in a prejudiced community will be found in substance elsewhere in this paper. The "conviction" is so obviously a judicial crime that one wonders how any worker learning the facts could [any] longer have respect for a judicial system that would tolerate such a procedure. The case of Ford and Suhr had its counterpart in that of the Chicago Haymarket victims of 1887. The atmosphere surrounding the prosecution and defense was similar in both cases. Both grew out of industrial conflicts which the employing class sought to stifle by force. Retaliation at Haymarket in 1886[2] resulted in the death of several policemen; self-defense of strikers at Wheatland in 1913 resulted in the death of a district attorney and a deputy sheriff. In both instances, tools of the employers were the aggressors; in neither instance was any attempt made to apprehend or punish those tools. On the other hand, in both cases the prosecution admitted that none of their would-be victims had actually committed murder, or used any murderous weapons; they had only CONSPIRED to murder, and must, therefore, be punished with death or life imprisonment. But "conspiracy" was not even remotely proven in either instance. The victims were simply railroaded to gratify the insatiable blood-lust of the employing class.

Nearly twenty-seven years have elapsed since the gallows strangled out the innocent lives of Parsons, Spies, Engel and Fischer.[3] Still, we have a repetition of the same thing in the life sentences imposed upon

Suhr and Ford at Marysville. During all those years, we American patriots have been duly impressed with the fiction about "equality before the law, one of the cornerstones of our free government." We have been told that "agitators" presuming to question the sanctity of "our courts and our judges and our juries" were "seeking to undermine the foundations of law and order." After the release of Haywood in 1907,[4] and of Ettor and Giovannitti in 1912[5], we were told that our accusations against courts as being "capitalist-controlled institutions" were proven to be unfounded; that all courts were simply mills for grinding out "equal and exact justice for all citizens." We answered that THE WORKING CLASS FREED HAYWOOD AND ETTOR, and insisted that otherwise their doom had been [sealed][6], as in the case of the Haymarket victims and others who have succeeded them through the judicial hopper. Now again, with Ford and Suhr behind the prison bars for life, we hurl the charge back [in] the teeth of those who convicted them: YOU ARE TOOLS OF THE EMPLOYING CLASS. You are the most dangerous [sort] of men to deal with the lives and liberties of workingmen; the most dangerous because you feel NO RESPONSIBILITY toward those whom you are trying. You are responsible only to their employers and those in sympathy with the bosses. Put a row of brass buttons on a brute with intelligence and feeling slightly above that of a gorilla only; make him understand that what he does to strikers or other workers in the name of "law and order," he does with impunity-and you have the record of police brutality against the working class since the beginning of the class struggle. Clothe a shyster lawyer in the "ermine of the judiciary," and keep his gaze directed toward the source of his emoluments of office, and he will twist the pure essence of the law to suit the material interests of the master class. Put an aspiring politician, no matter what he brands himself, in the legislature or the executive mansion, and he will religiously follow the game rules laid down for him by the economic masters.

There is no use bewailing or whining over these facts. To do so will not ease the lump on our cranium. What we of the working class must do is to recognize the judicial system, as well as the rest of the political paraphernalia, as parts of the repressive machinery of the master class, and act accordingly. We must bring to bear against that machinery and against capitalism as a whole the one all-powerful working class weapon-INDUSTRIAL SOLIDARITY. We must use all the weapons of defense and aggression that go with that solidarity. FOR ONE THING, WE MUST MAKE JUDICIAL CRIMES AGAINST WORKERS COSTLY IN DOLLAR AND CENTS TO THE MASTER CLASS. Up to the present, they have been costing us all the money and energy we could command. We must turn the bill in to the master, and see that he pays the same. We must recognize this is WAR, and that everything is fair in war-as the master class does. WE MUST BUILD UP THE ONE BIG UNION OF THE WORKING CLASS, which, by its organized power, will be able to slay the murderous hand of the enemy. The lives and liberty of Ford and Suhr, as well as thousands of other victims cry aloud (not to heaven, which is dumb) but to the working class of the world, from behind the cold walls of the Folsom penitentiary. They shall be heard!

The IWW's threat to coerce California into releasing Ford and Suhr by making it too expensive to keep them jailed was a serious one. Initially, during the summer of 1914, the Agricultural Workers' Organization organized pickets at the Durst farm, hoping to dissuade workers from harvesting the crop. Although this effort failed, the Dursts were forced to spend a sizable sum to pay for private guards and to install perimeter lighting.

Believing that the union could not sustain the level of mass action required to force the state to free Ford and Suhr, the IWW turned to sabotage as the primary tactic. During the winter of 1914-1915, the IWW escalated the threat level. Hundreds of thousands of stickers were printed by the California Wobblies and posted on highways throughout the state, especially in rural, farming areas. The stickers read:[7]

FORD AND SUHR MUST BE FREE!
Therefore a boycott is on against the Hop-Fields
Fruit Canners and All Ranching

Beware especially of all Canned Goods made in California

Hoboes know how to act

BEWARE
California Canned Goods
Don't stick copper nails or tacks in Fruit Trees or Grape Vines

IT HURTS THEM

It seems unlikely that these stickers had any impact, beyond annoying the authorities. The following correspondence indicates that Haywood and the IWW leadership were well aware of the strategy being followed in California, and approved of it. Charles Lambert, a Scot, came to the United States in 1905. He worked as an unskilled laborer in oil fields and on construction sites, before joining the IWW in 1911. Lambert was soon elected to be the secretary of the Sacramento joint local. After the Wheatland incident, he served as the secretary of the Ford and Suhr Defense Committee in 1914-1915.

DOCUMENT FIVE
Letter
Charles Lambert to William Haywood

Joint Locals I.W.W. Sacramento, Calif.
1/22/15

Mr. Wm. D. Haywood
Fellow Worker:

Please find enclosed money order for $7.50 which will be part payment on the 100 dues stamps borrowed from headquarters before you took office. (This is local #334's account.) I have only 20 stamps left of them, so if you can let me have 50 more on credit, and also 50 dues books for #334, that will leave me still owing you for 100. I may be able to hustle some more of these accounts before the end of the month, but it is terrible hard pickings this winter.

In regard to that mistake of my local #334's quarterly report, it was merely a slight mistake in addition. I don't see how we all happened to let that slip. I will correct it in the monthly report by putting it in as mistake in addition, $1. Will also correct in next quarterly report, if I am here.

Things are going along quietly in the Ford and Suhr cases at this time. The hearing for the pardon comes up before the Governor about the middle of next month.[8] A definite date has not been set yet. It has been decided that there will be no petitions circulated throughout the state for signatures, but instead the Labor Council of Frisco and the State Federation of Labor are circulating all the labor organizations in the state asking them to send a delegate from their local union to represent them when the hearings come off. They think this will have more bearing on the Governor than a mass of signatures would have. If all the locals send a delegate, which, of course, they won't, but if a fair percentage do, there would be a quite good sized gathering.

I was in Frisco Saturday and Sunday and talked with McNutt[9], the lawyer whom the A.F. of L. hired to write the petition for pardon, and he said that there were only two things that he was afraid of, and they were that the Governor might either take the case under advisement for a while and might let it ride for a year, or he might try to play both sides of the string and cut the sentence down to five or ten years.

I was also talking to George Speed[10] while there. He does not put any faith in Johnson's goodness whatever, and believes, like myself, that only a sufficient show of force will make him come through the way we want.

Hoping for a favorable reply in regard to the dues stamps, and dues books,

I remain yours for the One Big Union,

C.L. Lambert, Secretary

P.S.: Would also like to know price and date for E.G. Flynn lecture.

IWW Trial Transcript, pp. 10942-44

DOCUMENT SIX

Letter

William Haywood to Charles Lambert

Jan. 26, 1915

Mr. C.L. Lambert
Secy. No. 334
114 Eye St.
Sacramento, Cal.

Fellow Worker:

Your letter of the 22nd inst. Enclosing money order for $7.50 at hand. Find enclosed, herewith, receipt for the amount which has been credited to the account of Local 334 as follows:

On account dues stamps----$7.50

This is an account of the 100 dues stamps advanced you some time ago.

Your request for 50 dues stamps and 50 dues books on credit, noted. Dues stamps are enclosed herewith, and the dues books mailed by Parcel Post this date.

Note that you will correct the quarterly report.

I see the action being taken in the case of Ford and Suhr. I think as you do that there will be little accomplished unless we can demonstrate the fact that we will be on the job everywhere until those boys are released.

I will let you know in the very near future as to price and date of the Flynn lectures.

With Best Wishes, I am
Yours for Industrial Freedom
Wm. D. Haywood,
Gen. Sec'y-Treas.

IWW Trial Transcript, pp. 10945-46

On March 5, 1915, Governor Hiram Johnson held a hearing to consider the cases arising out of the Wheatland incident. The IWW was convinced that Johnson was biased and that it was, therefore, necessary to further escalate the threats. The following summer, the IWW adopted a different tactic, attempting to pressure Johnson by issuing nebulous threats to torch California's agricultural fields. Charles Lambert told a reporter from the Hearst newspaper chain, "We don't care what the papers print about the organization in regard to incendiary fires. But Ford and Suhr must be free."[11]

There is no credible evidence that anyone deliberately set fires during the harvest season of 1915. Nevertheless, it is clear that IWW leaders hoped that such fires would be set. Although the union did not direct its members to engage in arson, signals were clearly being sent encouraging rank-and-file Wobblies to act on their own by delivering a blow for Ford and Suhr.

The following correspondence indicates that those in the union's headquarters, including Haywood, not only knew of these arson threats, but approved of this as a viable strategy.

DOCUMENT SEVEN

Letter

Vincent St. John to Charles Lambert

Chicago, Ills., May 10th, 1915

Mr. C.L. Lambert
Secy. No. 71
114 I. Street
Sacramento, Cal.
Fellow Worker:

Your letters of the 4th and 6th inst. at hand. Copy of bill creating Board of Pardons, which you enclosed also, noted.

In my judgment, you have sized up the Governor's course of action, and he will no doubt be able to get away with it, so far as the voting wage slave is concerned. The only thing upon which we can rely is the power of the I.W. W. to cut into the profits of the California employing class to such an extent that they will instruct their servants in the State House to release Ford and Suhr.

Am sorry that the local is up against it, and that conditions would not permit taking a chance on Flynn meeting. Note your visit to Ford and Suhr, also passage of the bill, and plans for trying to secure a new trial on [the] basis of information you have in the form of affidavits.

With reference to Local Union No. 78, will state that charter for same was granted to a local at Franklin, Mass., shortly after the Lawrence strike. We never heard from them since the charter was granted.

Fellow Worker Haywood has been called to Washington, D.C. by the Industrial Relations Commission, and will be gone [for] six or seven days.[12]

With Best Wishes, I am
Yours for Industrial Freedom,
Vincent St. John, Acting Secretary

IWW Trial Transcript, pp. 10973-4

DOCUMENT EIGHT

Letter

Charles Lambert to William Haywood

Joint Locals I.W.W.
114 Eye St., Sacramento, Calif.
August 14th, 1915

Mr. Wm. D. Haywood

Fellow Worker:

Yours of the 11th at hand and contents noted, and in reply will state that we will give it a trial as soon as we can get hold of some stickers. We gave all we had away, and will have to write to some of the Locals and get some from them; the scheme looks like it would work fine alright.

We had a visit from the secretary of the Immigration and Housing Commission yesterday, and we filled his ear aplenty.[13] He told us of a big firm in England having cancelled an order for over 150,000 cases of California fruit; he said he had no idea what had caused it. Well, we showed him samples of stickers that have been scattered all over England and Australia, and told him, besides, that we understood that the Kaiser had given strict orders to the German spies in this country to never let up on the burning of ranches and canneries in California until Ford and Suhr were freed; gave out a partial list of burnings in this state that totaled over $800,000.

Have sent the clipping to *Solidarity*, so you will see the full report of this guy's dream soon. Find enclosed a money order for $7.50, [and] two receipts signed by F.H. Little for a total of $7.50, $15 in all, for which send me 50 dues stamps for #334 and 50 dues stamps for #71.

Getting back to the article in the Bee, I might mention that Frank Little and I signed a statement for the Sacramento Union reporters, and it appeared in this morning's Union, in which we declared (as is the truth) that the I.W.W. has no "inner circle and that if any individual members had done any of this burning, they did not do so with the sanction of the organization."

I remain yours in the fight for the freedom of Ford and Suhr, and the O.B.U.

                        C.L. Lambert
                            Secretary

IWW Trial Transcript, pp. 10981-2

DOCUMENT NINE

Letter

William Haywood to Charles Lambert

Chicago, Ills. August 18, 1915

C.L. Lambert
Secy. No. 71.
114 Eye Street
Sacramento, Cal.

Fellow Worker:

Your letter of the 14th with money order for $7.50 and two receipts from Frank Little for money advanced him, $3.00 and $4.50, making a total of $15.00, in payment for 50 dues stamps for Local 334 and 50 dues stamps for Local 71, at hand.

Enclosed find receipts and stamps to cover the amount.

I note your interesting interview with the secretary of the Immigration and Housing Commission. The information he gave you was interesting.

I think it would be well to get a number of the copies of the *Sacramento Bee* and clip this story that you mention, and send it to different papers. The information that it contains will make news, and be good publicity anywhere.[14]

I have received a reply to my inquiry about John Raymond's card from Eureka, Cal. Fellow Worker Wahander says that nothing was left with the Finnish branch, with the exception of the charter, and that he knows nothing about the books or the card.

With Best Wishes, I am
Yours for Industrial Freedom
Wm. D. Haywood
Gen. Sec'y-Treas.

IWW Trial Transcript, pp. 10983-84

DOCUMENT TEN

Letter

William Haywood to Charles Lambert

INDUSTRIAL WORKERS OF THE WORLD
164-166 W. Washington Street, Room 307
Chicago, Ills., September Fifteenth, 1915

Mr. C.L. Lambert
Secy. Local Union #71
114 Eye Street
Sacramento, Cal.

Fellow Worker:

Yours of the 11th with money order for $4.95 in payment of thirty-three due stamps for Local #71 is received. Enclosed find receipt and stamps to cover the amount.

Your remittance for $15.00 came O.K. and the stamps were immediately sent to you.

The only paper that I have received from you recently is the Sacramento Star, containing a story saying that a pardon had been denied the boys and that the Governor had refused to consider the matter at all as long as sabotage was threatened.[15] It went further to say that there were mitigating circumstances that would justify the Board of Pardons in taking action, but that nothing would be done under the circumstances. I think this statement is an indication of weakness. It appears to me that the line up is good, and the agitation in behalf of Ford and Suhr should be continued stronger than ever. If a few big contracts are cancelled, it will do more than can be done in any other way.

Yours for Industrial Freedom,
Wm. D. Haywood
General Sec'y-Treas.

IWW Trial Transcript, pp. 10992-3

Threatening to burn California's crops was a perilous tactic, and it was soon dropped. In September 1915, Governor Johnson rejected the applications for pardon, insisting that he would not be intimidated by the "incendiarism" being threatened by the IWW. Soon afterward, the Agricultural Workers' Organization stopped its threats of arson, and turned, instead, to the more positive strategy of trying to organize California's migrant workers.

The IWW Reverses Its Position on Sabotage

As late as April 1917, just as the U.S. was declaring war on Germany, *Solidarity* boasted of the union's willingness to engage in sabotage in both a cartoon and an editorial.

The Cat Always Come Back
Ralph Chaplin
Solidarity. April 14, 1914

DOCUMENT ELEVEN

Editorial

Solidarity,

April 14, 1917

Sabotage is a weapon of industrial warfare. It is one form of striking, and, like any other method of striking, is primarily intended to "hit the bosses" in the pocketbook. Sabotage is just as necessary to the wage slave of today as were the bow and arrow to his prehistoric forebear. In seeking to "outlaw" sabotage, the legislators of the Western states are attempting to place human necessity outside of the law. But "necessity knows no law." They can just about as easily stop sabotage with legislation as a medicine man could stop a tornado with a tom-tom.[16]

Within a few months after this editorial in *Solidarity*, the General Executive Board reversed the organization's position and came out in opposition to sabotage. The following resolution was first printed in the *IWW's Defense News Bulletin* issue of May 4, 1918. Although the resolution as printed did not provide the names of those signing the resolution, a brochure issued by the union after the war had ended printed the resolution with the names of three GEB members, Francis Miller, Richard Brazier and Charles Lambert, as endorsers, along with a short statement from Haywood endorsing the resolution.[17] A note also explained that the document had been approved by the GEB prior to the indictment issued in Chicago on September 28, 1917 charging more than a hundred IWW leaders with a conspiracy to violate the Espionage Act. The absence of Frank Little indicates that the resolution was approved after August 1, 1917, the day he was assassinated. Furthermore, William Wiertola, the fifth member of the GEB during the summer of 1917, was one of those indicted who went underground in order to avoid being arrested. This would seem to indicate that the resolution was adopted by the GEB in August or early September 1917, shortly before the Chicago indictment was issued.

By the time the GEB acted, it was clear that the federal government was preparing to make the IWW a prime target for repression.

Haywood and the General Executive Board realized that the union's advocacy of sabotage would be interpreted as a call to violence, and would be used by the federal government as a convenient rationale for destroying the union.

The 1917 resolution was reaffirmed in 1919 by the General Executive Board composed of an entirely different set of members, and then adopted by the 1920 convention as well.[18]

DOCUMENT TWELVE

Resolution

WHEREAS the Industrial Workers of the World has heretofore published, without editorial adoption or comment, many works on industrial subjects, in which the workers have a natural interest, including treatises on "Sabotage", and

WHEREAS the industrial interests of the country, bent upon destroying any and all who oppose the wage system by which they have so long exploited the workers of the country, are attempting to make it appear that "Sabotage" means the destruction of property, and [that] the Industrial Workers of the World favor and advocate such methods, now

THEREFORE, in order that our position on such matters may be made clear and unequivocal, we the General Executive Board of said Industrial Workers of the World do hereby declare that said organization does not now, and never has, believed in or advocated either destruction or violence as a means of accomplishing industrial reform: first, because no principle was ever settled by such methods; second, because industrial history has taught us that when strikers resort to violence and unlawful methods, all the resources of the government are immediately arrayed against them and they lose their cause; third, because such methods destroy the constructive impulse which it is the purpose of this organization to foster and develop in order that the workers may fit themselves to assume their place in the new society, and we hereby reaffirm our belief in the principles embodied in the Report of this body to the Seventh Annual Convention, extracts from which were later republished under the title, "On the Firing Line."

Violence

Questions involving the use of violence presented the IWW with a series of difficult problems. The union functioned within a context in which violence was commonplace. Corporations hired private security firms, which, in turn, employed gunmen to terrorize strikers. Local police frequently assaulted Wobbly organizers, sometimes severely injuring them. Furthermore, in the Western states where the IWW was most successful, guns were common and violence an integral aspect of daily life. Even unions affiliated to the American Federation of Labor, mainstream business unions, sometimes resorted to violence to win strikes.

At the grassroots level within the IWW, there was a pervasive belief that the union should be more willing to use violent tactics to rebuff attacks and to force corporations to grant concessions. Union leaders generally discouraged the use of violence on both strategic and theoretical grounds. They understood that government officials were looking for a convenient opportunity to crush the Wobblies. Any involvement with acts of violence would enable the authorities to cast union activists as a small band of terrorists who relied on violence because of their inability to convince workers to join their cause.

This was a position based on tactical prudence and yet one that made sense. IWW leaders were also convinced that the use of violence would hinder the union in achieving its long-run goal. A central tenet of the IWW's vision held that capitalism could not be reformed and that only a revolutionary transformation could provide the basis for a new society. (Most Wobblies viewed themselves as anti-authoritarian, radical socialists.) A central component of a revolutionary movement would be a strong, militant industrial union, the IWW, that could organize a general strike that would shut down the economy at the critical moment. The key to creating such a movement was a deepening of the solidarity of the working class and this could only be developed through mass action, primarily strikes and demonstrations.

Relying on force would inevitably lead to the creation of distinctive paramilitary units. The priority would then become the arming and drilling of these forces, leading inevitably lead to a minimizing of the need for building the union as a mass organization. Thus, during the summer of 1917, the union's heyday, the IWW organized effective strikes involving tens of thousands of workers on the basis of a strategy that actively discouraged the use of violence, and even went further, urging workers to avoid situations that could lead to violent confrontations.

Nevertheless, complex issues involving the use of violence frequently arose. The execution of Joe Hill in November 1915 infuriated Wobblies around the country, some of whom were convinced that the union needed to retaliate. Calls for the union to counter violence with violence came from rank and file Wobblies and even from those on the General Executive Board. Nevertheless, the union held firm to its belief that only a strong, militant workplace organization could provide a way forward.

Issues related to the use of violence were particularly salient in the drive to organize migrant farm workers. The Agricultural Workers' Industrial Union #500 organized farm workers traveling to harvest grain throughout the Midwest. Violence was endemic within this sub-culture and migrant workers often carried guns as protection against armed robbers. Unfortunately, this just added to the overall insecurity and fear. The AWIU tried to balance its concern for the safety of individual members with its goal of creating an environment that was safe for all and where violence had been eliminated.

Mass Action Versus Terrorism

A century ago, as now, one strain of anarchist thought held that the revolutionary movement could be advanced through acts of violence, the propaganda of the deed. Assassinations and terrorist acts were extolled as heroic deeds to be emulated. The first two documents reflect the concern within the IWW that some Wobblies were attracted to this vision. In 1914, Frank Cady, as secretary of the Portland local, wrote Vincent St. John, General Secretary-Treasurer, of the impact a local newsletter, *Justice*, was having on the local membership. St. John's response is a clear formulation of the IWW's commitment to mass action as an alternative to violent acts. His perspective was reflected in the position taken by IWW newspapers, but, as far as I know, his letter was never published.

DOCUMENT ONE

Letter

Frank Cady to Vincent St. John

Portland, Oregon, June 11, 1914

Vincent St. John
Chicago, Ill.

Fellow Worker:

Under separate cover I am sending you 2 copies of *Justice*, a free lance paper published in this town. The copies I am sending are supposed to be the Direct Action numbers. It is trying its utmost to get the endorsement of the local. If you will carefully read these papers you will see that they wish to substitute the military for economic organization. It places a false interpretation upon Direct Action. The average slave in reading this paper will get the idea that Direct Action means military tactics. We have been for 8 years trying to educate the workers along the lines of industrial organization. And, as I understand it, Direct Action means action taken by the workers through their industrial or trade organization to force concessions from the masters without recourse to any intermediary. This paper is making an attempt to transfer the activism of the workers from the industrial field to the military field. To my mind, the propaganda of this paper is of the most detrimental nature. For sake of illustration, we will say that in the very near future a strike breaks out in the lumber mills of this town. The lumberworkers get complete solidarity and thereby close up all the mills. The robber barons would be very foolish indeed if they did not use these two issues of *Justice* against strikers, and try to prove that Direct Action means nothing more or less than murder, arson and dynamite. In that way, the masters would be enabled to create such a sentiment that the strikers would be unable to offset. In other words, this paper with its propaganda will be instrumental in leading the workers to a shambles. In fact, their speakers from time to time have stated from their soap boxes that it was not necessary for the workers to organize, and they leave the impression on the minds of the slaves that all that is necessary for the slaves to do in order to overcome their masters is to get several rounds of ammunition and proceed against their enemies. Of course, myself, or any other well-informed rebel knows that dynamite, fire and other methods of terrorism at times are necessary in the class war. The reason I am writing this letter is that some of our members are inclined to fall for this stuff. Now, I would be well pleased if you would reply to this letter, and let me know by return mail your candid opinion of this paper, and also what our attitude should be towards it. Take your time and write us a good letter as we may need your advice on the matter before long. Hoping that you may see fit to reply to this letter in the near future, I remain

Yours for Industrial Power
Frank Cady

IWW Trial Transcript, pp. 10736-8

DOCUMENT TWO

Letter

Vincent St. John to Frank Cady

June 16th, 1914

Mr. Frank Cady
Sec'y 92
309 Davis Street
Portland, Oregon

Fellow Worker:

Yours of the 11th inst. at hand. Copies of *Justice* at hand and have read the same over. The direct action number of Justice reached me before, as the publishers of the paper have placed this office on the exchange list.

After reading the direct action number, I considered the proposition of writing an article in reply to the position taken by Justice. In view of the fact that Burns had already written me when the publication first started, requesting articles from time to time, I thought it would be a good plan to take advantage of his invitation in order to counteract the effect of the stand taken by the paper in advocating military tactics. I refrained from doing so because on further consideration I did not want to identify myself in the discussion of organization matters through the columns of a free lance publication. I did not think that very many, if any, of the active members of the I.W.W. would fall for the freak ideas expressed in the articles in question.

As far as my opinion of the paper is concerned, will state that after carefully reading all of the copies that have reached me I cannot see where the paper is of any value to the wage workers. The paper is a kind of journalistic hash endeavoring to cater to every kind of opinion in the radical and revolutionary movement. A publication of this kind has no educational value, the only effect that it can have is to confuse instead of educate its readers, especially where the readers may not have had very much experience with the revolutionary movement.

Military organization on the part of the workers would prove no more successful in that respect than it has for the employer. It is useless to argue that such an organization on the part of the workers would be workers and therefore in possession of the knowledge needed to operate industry. The army and militia and police are also workers for the most part, but their function is not, and never can be, to produce. While it might be possible for the workers to overthrow the existing government by a military program, the only effect so far as the working class are concerned, would be that they would overthrow one set of exploiters and set up in their place a new regime based upon the military power that would be generated during the struggle.

In short, the only result of success with a military program would be a change of masters, the same as in the case of a successful parliamentary program. Control of industry can never be made operative for the benefit of the workers except that the working class is organized for the purpose of controlling and operating industry for their own benefit. Such an organization does not need a military program and in fact is so far superior to such a program that it will be able to render harmless a military organization of the employing class once it has obtained even partial control in the basic industries of the country. It is true that while endeavoring to form this organization the workers from time to time may have to resort to the use of arms in defense of their lives.

The dangerous part of this proposition is that wherever a successful fight is made under those conditions, freaks of all kinds immediately take the exception to try to make it a rule. Furthermore the use of military tactics would not be necessary in Colorado or in any other struggle were it not for the fact that the labor movement of this country does not attempt to function in the manner that it should in order to prevent such occurrences at Ludlow, Calumet and other points where strikers are forced to clash with armed guards.

In the Colorado case,[1] the U.M.W.A., the organization that is interested, has it within its power to stop the production of coal in the

United States and were its members educated so as to appreciate the necessity of this line of action, they would not have had to fight with rifles at Ludlow. A mere threat of a general stoppage of coal production in the U.S. would have been far more potent than all of the ammunition expended in getting militia and gun men in that section.

Military program must be judged by the same rules as any other, that is power. While the strikers at Ludlow are able to successfully contend against the company's gun men, when the state militia and the superior mechanism of the U.S. military Force appeared upon the scene their military organization was forced to bow to the superior power of the Federal troops. Success then with the military program means that the workers have to provide the finances necessary to bring into the field the organization that is superior in military power to the Federal Government. This means that you will have to meet them in the point of numbers of men, in the point of efficiency, of equipment, large guns, unlimited supply of ammunition and efficient trained core of fighting men. I am not going to take the time to figure this out in dollars and cents, but, if you care to do so, you can try, and [then examine] the appropriations made to support the U.S. Army, and you will have some basis from which to figure what the expense would be to the working class.

The same amount of money and energy expended educating the workers on how to control industry in their own behalf and form an organization for such a purpose would serve to build up this organization that would get results. It is just as foolish for the workers to expect that they can compete with the already perfected military machine of the government as it would be to imagine that we can compete the capitalists out of industry.

One thing is certain, the members of the I.W.W. must learn to weigh every proposition that is advanced for their consideration on the scales for the purpose for which they are organized. It is well for them to consider any and all programs which are brought to their attention, but before giving their adherence to them they should judge what is offered by some other measure than the ability of individuals to sling ink and coin phrases and twist facts in order to make them appear favorable to the workers.

>With best wishes, I am
>Yours for industrial freedom,
>Gen Sec'y-Treas.

IWW Trial Transcript, pp. 10738-743

Joe Hill

Joe Hill was one of the few Wobblies with a reputation that extended far beyond the IWW. A Swedish immigrant and an unskilled worker who held a variety of jobs as he traveled around the West, Hill became famous by setting ironic and radical lyrics to popular tunes of the day. The IWW published his songs in its Red Books, which were then sung on strike picket lines and hobo jungles. Hill was also a talented poet and artist.

In January 1914, Hill was arrested for participating in an armed attack on a grocery store in Salt Lake City that resulted in the death of two men. When arrested, Hill was recovering from gunshot wounds; he neither explained how he received these injuries, nor where he was at the time of the incident. The evidence was inconclusive, and exactly what happened that day and who was involved in the armed assault at the grocery store remain unclear to this day. Hill was convicted of murder in a trial of doubtful validity and sentenced to death. In spite of an international campaign to gain a reprieve, Hill was executed on November 19, 1915. Among his last words were the phrase, "Don't waste time in mourning. Organize."

During the time he was held in jail awaiting the results of various legal appeals, Hill contributed several items to *Solidarity*, including a cartoon, an article and a poem.

IWW Submarines are Annoying the Enemy Everywhere
Joe Hill, *Solidarity,* October 24, 1914

DOCUMENT THREE

Article
Solidarity
December 19, 1914

I see in the "Sol" that you are going to issue another edition of the Song Book, and I made a few changes and corrections, which I think will improve the book a little, which I am enclosing herewith.

Now, I am well aware of the fact that there are lots of prominent rebels who argue that satire and songs are out of place in a labor organization, and I will admit that songs are not necessary to a movement. But I think that our little Song Book is doing good work for the cause; and whenever I "get the hunch," I intend to make some more foolish songs, although I realize that the class struggle is a very serious thing.

A pamphlet, no matter how good, is never read more than once, but a song is learned by heart and repeated over and over; and I maintain that if a person can put a few, cold common sense facts into a song, and dress them (the facts) up in a cloak of humor to take the dryness off of them, he will succeed in reaching a great number of workers who are too unintelligent or too indifferent to read a pamphlet or an editorial on economic science.

There is one thing that is very necessary in order to hold the old members interested in the class struggle, and that is entertainment. The rebels of Sweden have realized that fact, and they have their little blowouts regularly every week. And on account of that fact, they have succeeded in organizing the female workers more extensively than any other nation in the world. The female workers are sadly neglected in the United States, especially on the West Coast, and consequently we have created a kind of a one-legged, freakish animal of a union, and our dances and our blowouts are kind of stale and unnatural on account of being too much of a "buck" affair; they are lacking the life and inspiration which the woman alone can produce.

The idea is to establish a kind of a social feeling of good fellowship between the male and the female workers that would give them a little foretaste of our future society, and make them more interested in the class struggle and the overthrow of the old system of corruption. I think it would be a very good idea to use our female organizers, Gurley Flynn[2] for instance, EXCLUSIVELY for the building up of a strong organization among the female workers. They are more exploited than the men, and John Bull is willing to testify to the fact that they are not lacking in militant and revolutionary spirit.

By following the example of our Swedish fellow workers, and paying a little more attention to entertainment with original song and original stunts and pictures, we shall succeed in attracting and interesting more of the young blood, both male and female, in the One Big Union.

During the last days of his imprisonment, Hill wrote a poem expressing his continuing belief in a working class movement that could bring about a new society.

DOCUMENT FOUR

Poem
Solidarity
November 27, 1915

Workers of the World Awaken
Workers of the world, awaken!
Break your chains, demand your rights
All the wealth you make is taken
By exploiting parasites
Shall you kneel in deep submission
From your cradles to your graves?
Is the height of your ambition
To be good and willing slaves?

If the workers take a notion
They can stop all speeding trains
Every ship upon the ocean

They can tie with mighty chains
Every wheel in all creation
Every mine and every mill
Fleets and armies of the nation
Will at their command stand still

Join the union, fellow workers
Men and women, side by side
We will crush the greedy shirkers
Like a sweeping, surging tide
For united we are standing
But divided we will fall
Let this be our understanding-
"All for one and one for all."

Workers of the world, awaken!
Rise in all your splendid might
Take the wealth which you are making
It belongs to you by right
No one for bread will be crying
We'll have freedom, love and health
When the Red Flag is flying
In the workers commonwealth

The following poem by a rank and file Wobbly is indicative of the intensity of feelings evoked by the campaign to prevent Hill's execution.

DOCUMENT FIVE

Poem
Solidarity
November 20, 1915

"To the Governor of the Sovereign
State of Utah"
Joseph O'Carroll
We have decreed and you reply to us!
We had decreed and this is your reply:
"According to due process of Our Law—
"According to Our Code, Joe Hill must die.

"He has been given trial by his peers;
"By them found guilty and so he must pay
"The Law's exact and equitable debt—
"And he must die."
      Ah, this is what you say.

Must die! Ah, so consider just awhile
Our answer to your answer, and be still:
"We have examined all your evidence,
"And by our code we ask you for Joe Hill;

"For all your evidence perjured as palpably
"As any evidence by Pilate heard!
"Even by these your dull Iscariots
"No proofs of guilt adduced!
      No, not a word.

"Heard by your hirelings. (Ah, no, not you
"For you are the exception.) Pardon me!
"For you are just and no doubt independent—
"And for these reasons you will set Hill free.[3]

"Let in to the void recess of your skull,
"Your phantomed skull, a little of the truth,

"Of justice, unbiased, unblindfolded,
"Such as you may have dreamed of in your youth.

"Now Hill is guiltless by our edict passed
"Unanimous the verdict of his peers!
"We do proclaim his freedom from this crime
"For which you wish to shoot him it appears!

"Of course, he is unquestionably guilty
"Of stirring youth's swift coursing blood with song,
"With rebel chants of laughter and of love
"And rebel chants of hate.   Ah, this is wrong!
"Admitted for the sake of argument
"But listen! Whisper just a little while
"'Tis not a hanging matter even now
"To sing a song of hatred as you smile.

"Consult your Blackstone and his kindred crew
"Interpreters of this you call the Law
"Recall all your forensic platitudes
"All the drab precepts."
                    Is This What You Saw?

On any page or sentence in these books
Devoted to this law's interpreting:
"He shall be shot or hanged or imprisoned
"Who shall have the audacity to sing."

"Go slowly, Sir! Go slowly yet awhile.
"Be just, just Sir—-And, if you must, why frown
"Or weep or pray—But do not take their pay—-
"For there's a jungle just this side of town.

"Strange beasts, unkempt and gaunt which you and yours
"Have famished to satiety of Hate

"Unsatisfied, are in this jungle town.
"Beware good Sir—or it may be too late!

"They know Joe's songs! Ah sir, these beasts of prey
"They sing Joe's songs! Can I say more?-- And yet
"Tomorrow, if he's dead you'll feel and know
"Tonight, you merely glimpse a silhouette."

The IWW was convinced that Joe Hill had been framed, and that the mining corporations active in Utah were behind the plot to kill him. The following cartoon reflects this viewpoint.

The Firing Squad with the Screen Removed
Ralph Chaplin, *Solidarity*, November 27, 1915

The IWW's failure to prevent the execution was a bitter defeat. Wobblies were certain that Hill was innocent, and that he had been framed by the police. Many believed that the union should retaliate in kind. The following interchange involved two of the most prominent IWW leaders. Richard Brazier was born in England, and emigrated to Canada at the age of twenty, where he was employed as a railroad construction worker. He moved to Spokane in 1907 and joined the IWW a year later. A militant Wobbly, Brazier became secretary of the Spokane joint local in 1914 and a member of the IWW's General Executive Board in 1916. He also contributed several songs to the first edition of the IWW's songbook.[4]

Big Bill Haywood was a legendary figure who greatly influenced the course taken by the IWW. Haywood began working in the silver mines of Nevada at the age fifteen. He soon became active in the Western Federation of Miners and was elected its secretary-treasurer in 1900. Haywood was instrumental in establishing the Industrial Workers of the World, serving as the chair of its founding convention in June 1905. After having been acquitted on the charge of killing Frank Steunenberg, the former governor of Idaho, in February 1906, Haywood traveled around the country speaking for the Socialist Party. His election to the Socialist Party's National Executive Committee in 1912 marked a tremendous victory for the left-wing. Haywood was recalled from office in February 1913 on the basis of his advocacy of sabotage. He then returned to the IWW as General Organizer and was elected General Secretary-Treasurer in November 1914.[5]

The interchange between Haywood and Brazier reflects a broader debate within the IWW. Nevertheless, most Wobblies remained convinced that mass action provided the only meaningful response to state violence.

DOCUMENT SIX

Letter

Richard Brazier to Ben Williams

[November 19, 1915]

IWW Publishing Bureau
Cleveland, Ohio
Fellow-Workers:

Please find enclosed herewith M.O. for $2.50 in payment for B.O. #306 and two subs, also enclosed. I suppose you are informed by now of the successful ending of the Spokane Free Speech Fight. We won practically everything we fought for, we won the best location in town to speak, we also forced the city to revoke their obnoxious ruling that we must first obtain the written consent of the business man or property owner in front of whose place of business we wanted to talk, before the city would grant a permit to talk. Also, we gained the unconditional release of all prisoners in jail, something we did not gain the last fight here. The fight, short as it was, had the effect of reviving the locals very much. Last week being the banner week of the year for us.

I wonder what action we are going to take now that Joe Hill is shot.[6] We cannot afford to lay down on any such terrorist methods as they have used in Utah. We must retaliate some way, and frankly between you and I, I believe a little terrorism on our part, and not so much passive resistance, would gain us more results. There are times when the Mosaic code should be enforced by us, and the case of Joe Hill calls for retribution of the "eye for an eye" etc. kind.[7] Hoping that things are coming good for Sol. I remain, yours for the I.W.W.

Richard Brazier,
Sec'y I.W.W. locals
Spokane, Wash.

IWW Trial Transcript, p. 18751

DOCUMENT SEVEN

Letter

William Haywood to Richard Brazier

Nov. 23rd, 1915

Richard Brazier
115 Browne St.
Spokane, Wash.

Fellow Worker;

Yours of the 19th is received. It is good news to hear that you have gained the main contention in your fight for free speech. Almost as great as this is the fact that all prisoners are to be released unconditionally. It shows that we are, at times, able to make them compromise on what they call the law.

When we are organized enough to control economic power there is much of the law they will have to forget.

In Saturday last, I mailed you and all the locals a bulletin which I trust you will receive in time to arrange a meeting at 10:30 Thursday morning, November 25th.[8]

With Best Wishes,
Yours for Industrial Freedom,
General Sec'y-Treasurer

IWW Trial Transcript, p. 18752

Violence and Migrant Workers

Migrant farm workers were poorly paid, living close to subsistence levels. They rode on freight car trains as they traveled from one harvest area to another. Often they slept in informal camps, called jungles, in isolated areas near the railroad yards where they could jump the next freight car to where they were going. The IWW's Agricultural Workers' Industrial Union #400 organized migrant workers as they moved along these informal networks. As they did so, the union had to confront numerous problems, including the many threats of violence that threatened migrant farm workers.

Armed bandits hopped freight trains and proceeded to rob the harvest workers on them. In response, the union organized defense squads as protection. Defense squads also made sure that everyone on a freight train carried an IWW card, or joined on the spot. Those who refused were pushed off the train when it slowed down. Unfortunately, some squads went further, insisting that all of the migrant workers on the freight train who were not carrying the red card surrender their possessions before being dumped off the train.

The first set of documents in this section concerns the publication of an article that appeared in *Solidarity* in 1916 and that sought to address this last problem. It was written by Forrest Edwards, a veteran IWW member who had been active in the first concerted effort to organize farm workers during the harvest season of 1915. Edwards was elected the union's secretary-treasurer in 1916, and his article reflected the position of the AWIU. He found Haywood far more reluctant to confront this issue.

DOCUMENT EIGHT

Letter

Forrest Edwards to William Haywood

January 6, 1916
Des Moines, Iowa
414 E. Fifth St.

Mr. W.D. Haywood

Fellow Worker:

Enclosed please find 'MMS' on the subject "The Migratory worker and what he is up-against."

I mail this to you and ask you to forward same to *Solidarity* if you think it policy to do so. There is a demand in our organization for us to take a stand on this issue. The menace of the High-Jack and Gambler and Boot-legger to our effort is hardly understood except [by] one

[who] has been on the job. This question is sure to come up at our next meeting in K.C. Most of the members are in favor of us taking a stand. It will be best in my opinion to run such an article as I have written, previous to admitting that there are any of these in the organization. They will see the handwriting on the wall. They will have to do one of two things.

I could have went more into details on the subject but I understand it to be a ticklish issue. Anyway, look it over and if you approve of its publication, send it on to Williams.

Yours for One Big Union
Forrest Edwards

IWW Trial Transcript, p. 5168

DOCUMENT NINE

Letter

William Haywood to Ben Williams

Jan. 13, 1916

Ben G. Williams
112 Hamilton Ave.
Cleveland, Ohio

Fellow Worker:

Enclosed find manuscript from Forrest Edwards. This is the first little note that has been struck against the Highjack. There may be a few of this element among our membership, but the fact does not want to be emphasized at this time. The Highjack is a hold-up, and the fellow workers from the harvest fields tell some great stories about their method of working. All during the last season, while many scissorbills were held up and robbed, not an instance is recorded of where an I.W.W. suffered this treatment. In many instances the Highjacks would say when they approached a crowd of workers, "All you fellows with red cards step over here," and would then proceed to go through the rest. This is not altogether new. I have known cases in the West when a strike was on, where the scabs would never get home with their pay. One might have called the hold-ups Highjacks, but there were good union men just the same. However, there is nothing strong in this article of Fellow Worker Edwards, and I send it on to you as he requests.

> With Best Wishes, I am
> Yours for Industrial Freedom,
> General Secretary-Treasurer

IWW Trial Transcript, pp. 5169-70

DOCUMENT TEN

Letter

William Haywood to Forrest Edwards

Jan. 13, 1916

Fellow Worker:

The manuscript on "The Migratory Worker and What He Is Up Against" is received. I turned it over to the editor of *Solidarnos*. He has made a translation for the next issue of the Polish Paper. Today I am sending it to *Solidarity*; expect that it will appear before long.

I feel that there are questions involved that ought to be considered with great care, and I do not believe that they should be discussed at the business meeting in K.C. or for that matter in any other business meeting. But it is something that should be talked over, and a line of action determined upon by the Organization Committee. There are some good men who have been temporarily side tracked, but who will again get on the main line when they see that the Organization means business. And there are some of those men whom we do not like to antagonize. They are red-blooded, and will make good members when they get on the job.

> With Best Wishes, I am
> Yours for Industrial Freedom,
> General Secretary-Treasurer

IWW Trial Transcript, pp. 5170-71

DOCUMENT ELEVEN

Article
Forrest Edwards
Solidarity
January 22, 1916

Migratory Workers and What We Are Up Against

This subject has been on my mind for some time, and only now have I decided to write on it. In the following paragraphs there will be no attempt made at moralizing about any of the many trades and professions common among the migratory population. Just a simple recognition of their existence together with their relations to the workers and the IWW, leaving the question of good and bad to the reader to decide for himself.

It will be impossible to discuss the migratory workers without at the same time bringing into the argument all of the migratory population. This course will be necessary for the reason that not all of the migratory population are migratory workers. There have been many attempts at writing and lecturing on the subject, but so far as I have been able to read or listen, none of the writers or lecturers were able to discuss the subject intelligently. This for the reason that they lacked the experience necessary to [gain] knowledge of the subject, or they were playing to the galleries. In either case, the result was the same. The real facts in connection with the life of the American hobo have been improperly assembled, or were not known to the author. The result has been confusion.

For a clear understanding of the "migratory worker," suppose we classify the migratory population. In doing this, I believe it best to use a term that will cover the migratory population. Take the term "Hobo." By using this term in a general sense, it makes our subject more easily understood. The term "HOBO," so far as this article is concerned, will apply to all of the migratory population.

Then for the sake of clearness, the hobo will be again subdivided into three classes. Under these three subdivisions we will proceed to discuss the hobo. They are as follows: "The Tramp," the "Crook," and the "Migratory Worker." Under these subdivisions, we will proceed to discuss the Hobo.

The Tramp

The tramp appears in many forms. That is, he has many different professions. He may be seen as a "Tinker," a "Mush-Fakir," a "PEDDLER," or an "AGENT." He may be a "Professional Bum." There are many such professions that cannot be classed with those followed by the Crook. The Tramp is a man that is up and busy. He depends upon his wits for his living. He is distinctly an individualist in thought and action. He is fighting the world alone. He is seldom found on a job of work. If he works at all for wages, he does so only as a means of getting himself started up in business. He does not depend upon wages for his bread and butter. The tramp is not interested in the matter of better wages, shorter hours of labor, or better working conditions. Moreover, he is no force for improved conditions except as he might talk favorably for them. The IWW has made no appeal to the tramp.

The Crook

Without stopping to argue whether this element is good or bad, we will simply recognize the fact that they are here. They form no small part of the migratory population. Their forces are being fast recruited. There are many of these new recruits who are but amateurs at the business. Although their sands are sent over the road every year, it seems that this method of dealing with them is no remedy for the profession. But aside from that, the Crook is bound to float around over the country with other hobos for practically two reasons. First, he is forced to change locations on account of his reputation. To avoid the Officers, and so on. Second, he must search new fields for exploitation. In the harvest belt, he follows the migratory workers from Oklahoma to Canada. He always has his eye open for easy money. When the workers leave, then he leaves also.

The Crook is a man who has decided to get along without working for wages. He appears as a "Professional Gambler," a "Boot-Legger," a "Confidence Man," or a "High-Jacker." He is known as "John-Yegg," a "Forger," and a dozen other such professions too numerous to mention. He depends upon his knowledge of these professions to get him his pork-chops. The remarkable fact to note in this connection is that few of them succeed in getting by any better than the wage-worker does. You will find them on the bum, as a rule.

This element is a real menace to the workers who depend upon their daily wages for their daily living. They are a bar to successful organization. They come into the Union of the workers, and get a card under the guise of being wage workers. They use their Union affiliation as a means of covering up. To escape attack. To get a degree of protection. And to further their exploits. The crook is not looking out for the welfare of the workers. He is looking out for himself. His motive is always personal gain. He is no force for higher wages and better working conditions because he does not operate on the job. If all of the Crooks in the world were organized, they would not function on the job, and consequently could not raise wages. They are not interested in job conditions. The IWW has no message for them. They are exploiters of labor.

The Migratory Workers

The migratory workers are Hobos, but all hobos are not migratory workers. The roaming nature of the migratory worker is developed more by reason of the seasonal work in different sections of the country upon which these men depend for their living. They are found in the harvest field of the north in the fall. In the oil fields of the south in the winter. Or they may be found in the Orange groves of California or the woods in northern Minnesota, Michigan or Wisconsin. This is all seasonable work. Then again, the migratory worker is found on construction work, such as railroads, dams and electric construction jobs. The wages and conditions are usually bad on such work, because there is little or no organization among them. These poor conditions prohibit the workers from making "big stakes." General dissatisfaction prevails among them.

It is out of the ranks of the migratory worker that the "Professional Tramp" and the "Crooks" are recruited. Dissatisfied with their lot, and seeing no way of getting away from the insults of the Boss, they try to make a stand. The migratory worker is exploited to the limit by the boss, and not being inclined to lead a crooked life, he is unarmed, and, as such, is an easy victim for grafters; grafters that evolved out of his own ranks.

The migratory workers are expected to beat their way on the railroad. Their wages are not sufficient to pay their fare on the cushions. The railroad companies expect this method of travel from their employees. They employ ex-convicts who have turned stool pigeons in the pen as railroad detectives to shoot and club men for beating the road. The migratory worker is in constant fear. The whole world is against him. Some drink booze. If they will indulge in the use of alcohol, they become easy prey for the gambler and others. With the card shark, he has no show. He lacks the knowledge necessary to the profession.

The migratory worker is the only one who can function on the job. He is the only one who is interested in bettering conditions on the job. His actions on the job are prompted by a motive consistent with his interest as a wage worker. To him, the propaganda of the IWW has a real meaning. The IWW has a message for the migratory worker. It appeals to the wage workers, and asks them to unite for a common purpose. That purpose is higher wages and shorter hours, and the emancipation of the working class from all exploitation.

Railroad brakemen were among the skilled elite of the railroad workforce. One task assigned to brakemen was the policing of freight trains to ensure that migrant workers and hobos did not ride the rails for free. Some railroad brakemen were friendly to IWW members, and allowed them to remain on board. Others used force to eject migrant workers from the freight cars. A few brakemen began using their power to illegally extort money from harvest workers, creating a swindle that was bitterly resented by those victimized.

This set of documents concerns the case of one IWW member, James Schmidt, who had jumped a freight car to travel to harvest jobs in North Dakota. When Schmidt refused to pay to remain on the freight car, the railroad brakeman used force, precipitating a gun battle and the death of the brakeman. The IWW rallied to the defense of Schmidt, who was eventually freed.

The case raises a host of issues related to the use of violence. Many migrant workers carried guns, but it is not clear that this made them safer and yet it definitely raised the overall level of violence. The brakeman involved was certainly running a scam, but Schmidt might have been better advised to have just left the scene rather than confronting the brakeman, as did his companions. Finally, despite these troubling questions, and the general attempt by the AWIU to discourage violent confrontations, the union felt it necessary to uncritically defend the actions of a Fellow Worker.

DOCUMENT TWELVE

Letter

Jack Law to William Haywood

424 South Washington Street
Aberdeen, South Dakota
September 26, 1915

W.D. Haywood
Sec'y Treas. I.W.W.
184 W. Wash.
Chicago, Ill.

Fellow Worker:

In answer to your letter to James Riley of the 16th, I will try to give you the facts in the case as I have learnt them since my arrival here, and, as soon as I can get a copy of the evidence of the preliminary hearing, I will send the same to you. As they have no grand jury in this state, it takes very little evidence to hold a man over.

On the eighth day of this month, Fellow Worker James Schmidt, in company with several other fellow workers, were on their way north to work in the fields of North Dakota. They intended to travel over the C.N.W.[10] After going to the railroad yards and getting in a car that was empty, a brakeman by the name of Ross? C. Farrar jumped in the car and pulled a gun and told them to dig up two bits, and, when they told him that they were broke, he told them to unload, which they did. As soon as they got on the ground, they told the shack that they had union cards, and as they were union men he ought to let them ride. At this point in the conversation, the other fellow workers went towards the other end of the train and just turned around in time to see the shack fire at Schmidt. Then Schmidt pulled a gun and told the shack to put his gun away, and then the shack fired again right at Schmidt's head, and Schmidt shot back, hitting the shack in the stomach. Schmidt started to run, and got away to another town, and was working on a machine when the sheriff got him. This is the story he told on the stand.

The state has one witness in the jail waiting to testify, and at the preliminary [hearing] his story was in our favor. We are trying to locate the fellow workers that were with Schmidt.

Now in regards [to] the attorney Schmidt wants, while the fee seems big, I think we can come clean on this case. The atty. wants one thousand dollars as his fee and two hundred and fifty to spend as he sees fit.[11] I have had a talk with him, and his motto is to win any way possible. He has the reputation of being the best in this state, and, if what the people around here say is so, he is the goods. I think we can realize the money as all the men in the harvest are sore at the train crews in this part of the country, and, on account of the activity in the harvest, I think we can cut the buck. The comrades here have raised one hundred dollars, and I think I can get a couple of hundred more in the near future. The case is expected to come about the twentieth of next month, so that makes the time short.

This man Schmidt is just a new member. I lined him up in Kansas City just a month ago. He is paid till the first of February 1916, and, after paying his dues, he had one dollar and forty five cents left in his pocket. He said, "Well Jack, I guess I will go broke anyhow, so you might as well split this with Joe Hill and Ford and Suhr," and he gave the last cent he had to help others, which showed the fine type that he is.

We are getting out lists, and will send them all over the country in a few days. Of course, the railroad is going to prosecute the case to the limit, but we figure on winning before we go to trial, and then we are sure. So that means work quick and quiet. The only thing that might spoil the whole thing is [if] some irresponsible person gets in this district and starts something, but we will keep our eyes open.

Hoping this explains the case. I remain yours for the goods.

> J.A. Law
> Secy Pro Tem

P.S.: Send all mail to 424 South Washington St., Aberdeen; all money should be sent to JAMES RILEY AT THE ABOVE ADDRESS.

P.S.S. If this does not make it clear to you, write to me and ask any questions you may wish, and I will try and get the correct dope. On account of the harvest agitation, we think it best to try this case on its merits without bringing the I.W.[W.] into it. Just go as strong on the publicity as you can at that end of the line, but we will keep quiet here for the present. Hope this meets with your approval.

IWW Trial Transcript, pp. 12091-4

DOCUMENT THIRTEEN

Letter

Jack Law to William Haywood

424 So. Wash. St., Aberdeen, So. Dak.
Sept. twenty-third, 1915

W.D. Haywood
Sec'y Treas.
Chicago, Ill.

Fellow Worker:

Received your letter of the twenty-first, and contents noted.

In regards [to] the attorney and the seemingly big fee, will state that I think we can raise the sum in the fields at this time as all the sentiment is against this stick up game of the brakemen.

Of course, we will expect some outside help, and I feel sure that we will get it, as the membership all through the Middle West realize that we are going to make a fight that will establish a precedent, for this is the first case that has come up where a man has tried to defend himself against the brakemen, and the hold up guys that infest the harvest. On account of this, men will donate liberally for the defense.

What we are trying to get in to the heads of the members is that they must not get in any kind of a row here at the present time, either with the officials or the farmers, as the jury will be mostly farmers. At this writing, we stand pretty good, and must keep [it] that way.

Bill, I know what is going to happen to Hill, and that should be a lesson to the membership not to be so slow in coming to the assistance of their fellow workers. If at the start of that case, everyone on the ground would have got busy and hired the best atty, and paid him his price, I feel sure that Joe would have been free now.

We are going to play the game different here in this case. We will try the case purely on its merits, and won't stand for the Org. [the IWW] to be put on trial, for, if we do, we will lose as sure as fate. In fact, we will try and win the case out of court, and go to court merely to make it look dignified, as the atty puts it.Next week I am going on a hunting trip with Ware, and we will make all the jurors on the way, do you get me?

So far, some little money has come in and we expect more later.

The socialists here have raised one hundred so far. That is fine, and I think if you write to Ware occasionally he will do more. We are stopping at his house, that is Riley and me room there.

Say, I put your name on the defense committee for I know that it will have some effect, and didn't think you would have any objections. In fact, I put all the names on without asking the consent of the owner of them as there is nothing else to do. I am doing the best I can, and if we don't get too many irons in the fire at the same time I think we will win, and if anyone comes butting in on this case and starts to knock, we will sure hand them a package.

One fellow worker was arrested with a gun in his pocket the other day; we told him before it happened not to carry it in this town; he insisted and got pulled [while] in the jungle; the attorney [that] went got his card, and told him to deny that he was a member. We will try and get him off with a light sentence, but we can't afford to get a man's life in danger by having men arrested with a gun at this time.

Hoping you agree with the policy mentioned. I remain yours to the finish.

J.A. Law

P.S. Enclosed find a list of the jury as empaneled for this term of court; some of them are all O.K. Overlook mistakes as I am a dead poor writer.

Jack L.

James Riley

Enclosure: Keep this to yourself or be sure that it is a member in good standing that you show it to. This is a list of Jurymen that have been summoned in the County of Brown, City of Aberdeen, State of South Dak., and will try all criminal cases. If you are working for any of the names mentioned below, don't get in bad, but try and make a good showing for the I.W.W.

List of names with city and township follows.

IWW Trial Transcript, pp. 12096-99

DOCUMENT FOURTEEN

Letter

William Haywood to Jack Law

September Twenty-seventh, 1915

Mr. J.A. Law
424 S. Washington Avenue
Aberdeen, S.D.

Fellow Worker:

Have carefully noted the contents of your letter of the 23rd inst., and think with you that the boys will come through in the defense of Fellow Worker Schmidt. They all must have realized that a case similar to this was liable to have happened at any time.

As near as I can learn, Fellow Worker Schmidt was merely defending himself, and would likely have been shot, probably fatally, if he had not fired at the brakeman. The fellow workers in that vicinity will know that this is a time when they must be on their guard, and not get in bad repute with either the officers of the city or the farmers in that community.

I can understand your trip with Ware. I am mighty glad you got in touch with him. From the way he writes, he is made of the right kind of stuff. It was splendid on the part of the socialists there to raise the hundred dollars in such short order. Of course, it was alright for you to put my name on the defense committee. It might be the means of lining up some who would otherwise feel indifferent.

Have the list of jurors and have placed the same on file.

All the members of the G.E.B. have voted in the affirmative on your credential. Have not heard from Frank Little, but am sending credential in this letter.

Yours for Industrial Freedom,
General Sec'y-Treas.

IWW Trial Transcript, pp. 12101-2

SECTION TWO : KEY CONFRONTATIONS

The Bisbee Copper Strike of 1917

Copper was an essential commodity during World War I. Every ounce of copper produced was immediately purchased by the governments of the Allied Powers and then converted into brass shell cartridges for munitions and copper wires for use in ships and planes. As the mining industry prospered, and mine owners made immense fortunes, wages lagged behind increasing prices and safety precautions were ignored in the rush to maximize production.

The Western Federation of Miners (WFM)[1] had been organizing copper miners since the 1890s. Nevertheless, most mining districts were still unorganized in 1917, as mining companies bitterly resisted the efforts of the WFM, in spite of its affiliation with the American Federation of Labor and its eagerness to cooperate with management.

The United States mined more copper than any other country and Arizona produced more than any other state. Production was spread across several mining districts, but the most important site was Bisbee, close to the Mexican border. Arizona's miners had become increasingly dissatisfied with the timid leadership of Charles Moyer, the president of the Western Federation of Miners. Stymied in every effort to reform the WFM, miners turned to the IWW.

The IWW national conference in November 1916 set organizing copper miners as a priority. In January 1917, Frank Little was sent by the IWW's Chicago headquarters to serve as the lead organizer for the drive. He was aided by Grover Perry, as secretary of the newly chartered Metal Mine Workers' Industrial Union #800 (MMWIU). The two worked well together, directing an effort that soon became the cutting edge of Wobbly activity.

Perry had worked as a miner for eight years, including a brief stint in Bisbee in 1912. After joining the IWW soon after its formation in 1905, he became a dedicated militant, organizing maritime workers in Baltimore and on the Great Lakes. In January 1917, he moved to Phoenix, Arizona, where he served as the first secretary of the MMWIU, and coordinated the drive to organize Arizona's copper miners.[2]

Thousands of miners flocked to join the IWW. In part, this reflected the widespread and bitter dissatisfaction with Moyer and the WFM leadership, and yet it also reflected the increasing radicalization of the miners, a trend that had been developing for several years. In addition, the U.S. decision to enter the war in April 1917 was enormously unpopular among copper miners in the Western states and the WFM's enthusiastic support for the war effort did not sit well in Arizona's mining communities.

Copper-mining communities throughout the West were a combustible mix in the summer of 1917. Butte, Montana, led the way, as thousands of miners went on strike shortly after 168 were killed in a fire that swept through the Speculator mine on June 8, 1917. Bisbee's miners went on strike on June 27, shutting down the mines in solidarity with Butte. The strike was tightly organized by the Bisbee branch of the Metal Miners' Union, with pickets adhering to a strict discipline. IWW leaders were careful to ignore the provocative acts of corporate guards, police, and the local authorities.

Strikes spread throughout Arizona, as the IWW tried to shut down copper production and force the companies to negotiate. The Globe-Miami district, 200 miles northeast of Bisbee, produced nearly as much copper ore as Bisbee. Mass pickets shut down the key mines in both Globe and Miami, rendering it difficult to carry on basic maintenance. This provided the federal government with the rationale it needed to intervene. On July 5, 1917 federal troops were dispatched to the district. The strike slowly dwindled and the mines in the Globe-Miami district remained non-union open shops.

In Bisbee, the union maintained a tight discipline and the strike remained solid. Unable to break the solidarity of the miners, the mining companies organized a mass deportation of nearly 1200 striking miners on July 12, 1917.

Bisbee marked the highpoint of IWW organizing and the defeat of the strike represented a devastating blow to the union.

The Western Federation of Miners

Charles Moyer, the president of the Western Federation of Miners, was detested by Arizona's copper miners. They were convinced that he was too ready to cooperate with the employers and that he was unwilling to use the militant tactics needed to properly defend the rights of miners. Every effort by the Arizona district to influence the policies of the WFM, or to gain autonomy within it, was summarily rebuffed. Militants tried to replace Moyer with the leader of one of the Arizona locals. When Moyer was reelected at the union's July 1916 convention, an election victory of dubious validity, dissident miners insisted that the Arizona district of the union be granted greater autonomy in determining its affairs. Moyer and the executive board of the WFM proceeded to totally reject Arizona's demands in November 1916, infuriating the rank and file. The intense disaffection generated by this controversy provided the impetus for the IWW's successful organizing drive during the spring of 1917.

The following poem comes from a collection of letters between Frank Little and Grover Perry that was submitted by the prosecution to the Chicago conspiracy trial. Unfortunately, the author was not named, but it is unlikely that either Perry or Little wrote it. The poem's bitter sense of betrayal accurately reflects the feelings of many copper miners throughout Arizona.

DOCUMENT ONE

Poem

Unknown Miner

[Spring 1917]

The Western Federation of Miners

1.

They have ruined every mining camp
They have driven men from home
They have SCABBED upon their brothers
From Bisbee up to Nome
They have been the cause of more starvation
They have never won a strike

2.

If they meet a bunch of radicals
Who will stand up for their rights
They will side in with the Company
And help them in their rights
And if the Company needs some GUN MEN
To shoot down their fellow men
They send their applications
To the W.F.M.

3.

You may think that I am lying
In writing this stuff
Just write to Butte, Montana
And you will find it is no bluff
You will find that Charlie Moyer[3]
And the W.F. of M.
Helped the Anaconda Company
When they sent men to the PEN

4.

Now you men of Arizona
Have tried your very best

To get rid of Charlie Moyer
The LABOR FAKING PEST
But you know the outcome of your struggle
For you can not hurt the REPTILE
That's two thousand miles away[4]
        5.
Now to rid yourself of Moyer
Here is an easy plan
Come in and join the WOBBLIES
And be with us to the man
Come be a FELLOW WORKER
And you will find my words come true
When Charlie drops his piecard[5]
He will very soon drop you

IWW Trial Transcript, pp. 7973-4

Organizing Arizona's Copper Miners

The following article from *Solidarity* was written by Frank Little as he traveled around Arizona organizing miners. Little emphasizes fundamental IWW principles, such as the necessity for an industrial union that would shut down an entire industry rather than allow the miners in one district to confront powerful mining corporations on their own. In addition, Little focused on the six-hour day as a critical demand that pushed the limits of reform within the capitalist system. A century later, the eight hour day is still the norm, with an increasing number of full-time workers compelled to work long hours of overtime.

    Little understood that the call for a six-hour day was not the typical union demand. He was not organizing copper miners so that they could pressure the corporations into conceding small improvements in wages and working conditions. Little viewed the IWW as the organization that could spearhead a revolutionary transformation of society. The demand for a six-hour day would cut across industrial sectors, unifying a wide range of workers in support of a common program and would thus constitute an important step forward.

DOCUMENT TWO
Article
Frank Little
Solidarity, April 21, 1917

Jerome, Ariz,- The Metal Mine Workers' Industrial Union No. 800 of the I.W.W. is forging ahead in the Western mining camps. The miners have come to the conclusion that the men who work in the mines, mills and smelters are the ones who should be benefited by unionism, and not the boss or the labor-skate "union" official. In other words, the miners want a union that will look out for the interests of the WORKERS-an INDUSTRIAL union.

The I.W.W. is growing in this neck of the woods, while the old W.F. of M., the mine owners, business men, Burns, and other detectives, are working together to fight the onward march of the One Big Union. In spite of this crowd, we will soon have full control of the mining camps. The miners are joining; that's enough. The grafters don't matter.

The I.W.W. program here is a six-hour workday, two men on a machine,[6] instead of one (a thing the W.F. of M. in its twenty-four years of organization has not put into effect), and the universal strike, instead of the local strike. This means that when the miners of one locality strike, the miners of other localities will not continue to dig ore to fill the orders of the strike-bound mines, but will strike in unison, closing ALL mines down at once, leaving no chance for scabs-union scabs at least.

The W.F. of M. when they demand shorter hours, or rather when they ask their friend, the boss, for a shorter workday, always seek to justify their request by stating that miners will do more work and better work in eight hours than they can in ten. And they have always proven that statement to be a fact. One man will do more work in eight hours than three could do in ten hours twenty years ago. BUT THE BOSS AND NOT THE MINERS IS THE ONE WHO HAS GAINED. The I.W.W. is out to better the conditions of the workers, and the workers alone.

And the I.W.W. never tries to justify any demands made on the boss, because the worker is entitled to all that he has the power to take from the parasites of industry. We want the six-hour day in all mines, mills and smelters, not because we want to do more work in that time than before, but LESS WORK. We want to put more men to work, want more time for rest and study, more time to agitate and strengthen our organization, so that we can go after the four-hour day-and get it.

The W.F. of M., like the U.M.W. of A., ties up the miners with contract agreements that make them work hard for a certain period of time for a specific wage. In this way, they are tied hand and foot, for if the miners of another district go on strike, the contract-bound union will have to scab on them in order to live up to the contracts. The I.W.W. makes no contracts, but holds that miners have a right to strike at any time they have a chance to better their conditions, and, furthermore, that the time to strike is when the boss most needs the workers.

At present, the Industrial Pirates are preparing for war, but all class-conscious workingmen are determined to stay at home and fight their own battles with their own enemy-the boss. By doing so, they will gain for themselves shorter hours, better wages and working conditions, which is a lot more than the "blocks"[7] will get who go to Europe to fight the battles of the master class. Kick the bosses off your back. Organize for industrial freedom. Don't fight the bosses' battles: join the I.W.W. and fight your own.

F. H. Little

The following cable was sent by Little to Haywood immediately prior to the first convention of the Metal Mine Workers' Industrial Union #800, which was held in Bisbee. Again, Little singles out the six-hour day as the primary demand for a coming industry-wide strike.

DOCUMENT THREE

Telegram[8]

Frank Little to William Haywood

Globe, Arizona, June 12, 1917

Wm. D. Haywood
Room No. 307
164 West Washington Street
Chicago, Illinois

Federation trying the same here as at Jerome. Notify metal miners of every company to prepare for general strike for six hours, six days a week and six dollars a day. If I am wanted, wire Bisbee.

F.H. Little

Bisbee Goes on Strike

The IWW's organizing drive in Bisbee was the union's most successful organizing project. Bisbee was the key to Arizona's copper mining industry. Until early 1917, the mining companies had quashed every effort to unionize the five thousand miners who worked in the district. Nevertheless, miners flocked to join the newly chartered Metal Mine Workers' Industrial Union #800. Even the leaders of the Bisbee local of the Western Federation of Miners deserted and joined the IWW.

On June 27, 1917, Bisbee's miners went on strike. Only a few miners crossed the picket lines to return to work and the production of copper ore was drastically reduced. Picket lines were tightly disciplined, as the strike leaders made every effort to prevent a violent confrontation that would provide the federal government with an excuse to send troops.

The intense exhilaration experienced by the miners in Bisbee is reflected in the following report of the first day of the strike. A.S. Embree was a veteran miner and a committed Wobbly. He served as the informal liaison between the Bisbee branch and the headquarters of the MMWIU in Phoenix.

DOCUMENT FOUR

Letter

A.S. Embree to Grover Perry

Bisbee, Ariz. June 26, 1917

Grover H. Perry
Phoenix, Arizona

Fellow Worker:

Enclosed find demands made on the companies here today. These demands were drawn up by the executive committee (Sullivan, Payne, Webb, Davis, Embree) this morning and were presented to the three big companies about one o'clock.

Sherman, manager of the Copper Queen, refused to hear anything from the committee, tore up the typewritten copy of the demands we gave him and threw the pieces in the waste basket. We left the demands with Goring's secretary, notifying him that if we did not hear from him by phone by five o'clock we would consider they had refused the demands. Shattuck told us that he hoped he could settle differences with his own employees individually, but that he would have nothing to do with the I.W.W.[9]

A special meeting of the branch was held in the hall at three o'clock, at which the executive committee made their report. The meeting endorsed the action taken unanimously, and called a mass meeting to be held at the City Park for seven in the evening.

The mass meeting was a success beyond our best expectations. The speakers were all mud diggers who got up at a minutes notice and rivaled Bill Cleary at his best. By the way, we gave Cleary a chance, without begging him to speak, but he gracefully declined.[10] It was the biggest crowd we have seen yet in the park, and they seemed to be pretty solid with us. We dwelt on the necessity of going out while Butte was still on a strike, and while Globe and Miami were ready with their demands.

After the meeting one hundred odd applications were filled out and cards issued, and another special meeting was held in the hall, at which pickets were appointed to take charge of each of the shafts and urge men to keep away from the work. The way the bunch volunteered for picket work would make you feel good. Some of them even insisted in going to the change rooms to catch the night shift coming off work. We did not consider it good policy to attempt to pull off the night shift, as we were not organized for it, and we were afraid if we tried, and did not make a good job of it, it would have a bad effect on our work in the morning.

Before I forget it, I want to impress on you the need of stamps, application blanks and cards, in case you have forgotten them. Kimball[11] has been using the Spanish blanks after he ran out of the others.

The executive committee is still on the job (two A.M.), and will be working till noon before we can see a chance of getting away for a rest. Yes, and a mass meeting at the park has been called for one, so we will only have one hour to sleep. We have sent wires to the papers, to Haywood and all the branches we thought necessary.

Sherman went down in all the Queen shafts tonight and talked to the men.[12] The work they are doing underground is stulling[13] and cleaning up and taking out the tools. Several shift bosses are coming out with us. The only pumpman working at the Shattuck is out. The engineers are not to be counted on, but we think if we can get them to frame up demands for themselves, it will be possible to get most of them.

The Mexicans are almost a sure bet, as we are demanding a minimum of $5.00 for all topmen. Kimball got hold of a good man for organizer among the Mexicans and he is on the payroll.[14] We could not wait to consult you, as it was necessary to get immediate action. Six kids, nippers[15] on Sacramento Hill, came up to the hall and asked us what we wanted them to do. They said they would picket all the others, and would help with the Mex.

We wired Sheriff Wheeler[16] to take care of the bootleggers, and told him we would give him all the information we could so as to put them out of business.

WEDNESDAY 4 P.M.

As you have already been informed by phone, the calling out of the day shift was a great success. Many men were turned back on their way to the shifts by our pickets, and as each squad had a captain whose place it was to report the number of men who went to work at each shift, it did not take us long to get a line on them. The total number normally reporting for work at each of the shafts is 2700. The number reported by our pickets as going on shift is about 740. This would leave just under 2000 men who decided to stay with us. We expect a still better percentage from the night shift, as we have been drilling them all day and had a splendid mass meeting again at one o'clock in the park, all the speakers mud diggers.[17]

I am rushed for time, so cannot give further details and cannot touch just now on the other points you referred to.

>Yours for Revolution,
>A.S. Embree
>Press Committee

IWW Trial Transcript, pp. 8242-45

Bisbee's miners viewed the strike as an extension of the struggle that had begun in Butte, Montana, where miners had walked out after the deadly Speculator fire. Nevertheless, Bisbee's miners had their own specific grievances as embodied in the following set of demands.

DOCUMENT FIVE

Demands of the Bisbee Miners[18]

The undersigned committee has been appointed by the Metal Mine Workers' Industrial Union No. 800, Bisbee branch, to present to the Mining Companies of the Warren District the following demands:

First: The abolition of the physical examination.
Second: Two men to work on machines.

Third: Two men to work together in all raises.
Fourth: To discontinue all blasting during the shift.
Fifth: The abolition of all bonus and contract work.
Sixth: To abolish the sliding scale. All men underground [to receive] a minimum flat rate of $6.00 per shift. Topmen $5.50 per shift.

> Ben K. Webb, Chairman
> M.C. Sullivan
> W.H. Davis
> J.C. Payne
> A.S. Embree
> Chas. Tannehill

The Strike Spreads

As soon as Bisbee walked out, the MMWIU leaders understood that it was essential to win the strike, and that this could only be done by spreading it throughout Arizona. Perry sent organizers to mining districts throughout the state, and, indeed, to surrounding states, urging miners to support the Bisbee and Butte miners by crippling production.

Miners in several districts throughout Arizona went on strike. In the Globe-Miami district, the strike struck deep roots, with mass picket lines stopping all production. During the first days of the Bisbee strike, it seemed that the strike was gaining momentum, and victory seemed near.

The following letters from leaders of the Bisbee strike reflect the belief that the strike would be won, in part by spreading the strike throughout the Southwest and even to the iron ore district of the Upper Peninsula of Michigan.

DOCUMENT SIX

Letter

J. McDonald to Grover Perry

Bisbee, Ariz. 7-6-17

Grover Perry
Salt Lake City, Utah

Fellow Worker:

Just had a long distance phone from McGoshan in Jerome that the boys there had just come out on strike ninety percent strong, twenty-five hundred working there. We have sent a man to Ray today to pull the men there. The idea is to get them out, and line them up afterward. If you can get the men out in Bingham Canyon and Ely, we will pull out all of the Guggenheim interests in New Mexico and Arizona.

The Executive Comm. here thinks that the best thing to do now is to pull them out as quick as possible, and line them up afterward. It looks as if we would have the copper country lined up in a very short time. We asked Haywood to try and get the men out on the Michigan copper belt, if possible. We see in the *Bisbee Review*[19] this morning that the I.W.W. was holding meetings in Hancock, Mich. This looks more like the big drive into the trenches of capitalism every day.

Yours for the One Big Union,
J. McDonald
Press Committee

P.S.: Another letter encloses latest news from here. You got the letter the other day suggesting Pete Munyon who is now in Eureka, Utah to go to Ely. Kimball will write you today also.

J.McD

IWW Trial Transcript, p. 8252

DOCUMENT SEVEN

Letter
Bisbee Strike Press Committee to Grover Perry

Bisbee, Ariz. 7-6-17

Grover H. Perry
Salt Lake City

Fellow Worker:

Fellow Worker James Thompson just arrived in Bisbee this morning. Last night, [Stanley] Clark spoke to over three thousand in City Park.[20] Clark left for Globe this morning; the situation here is tip-top, victory is sure. The big industrial strike of the Metal Mine Workers, which is fast spreading over the entire West, has already shut down mines to the extent that copper production has decreased half a million pounds a day. Mexican topmen are all out, and over three hundred of them have lined up out of three hundred and fifty employed. Very few mechanics working.

The spirit of solidarity shown is remarkable. No disorder and no bootleg booze. These tactics are bringing the corporations to their knees, as they can find no excuse to use violence. Reliable reports from different parts indicate that many more districts will soon fall in line, and the entire copper industry will be shut down by the strike. The Metal Mine Workers' [Union] will soon get better conditions for the workers.

A parade advertised by the Copper Queen Corporation had only a small number of persons in line, a few muckers and bosses, the rest were children and business men from Douglas, Tombstone and Bisbee. An unusual feature was that the paraders had to do their own cheering as the few onlookers showed no enthusiasm for the Company tools. Sentiment and the power of organization is on our side. Assistance has been assured from various sources, as well as the A.W.O., the I.W.W. organization which controls the harvest fields.

The strike of the folded arms is winning. Our demands will soon be granted. Solidarity and intelligence will win; do your part.

                Yours for Industrial Freedom,
                Press Committee

IWW Trial Transcript, p. 8254

The Six-Hour Day

Frank Little had been signing miners into the MMWIU on the basis of a program that highlighted the demand for a six-hour day. On June 17, 1917, the first convention of the MMWIU #800 was held in Bisbee. Delegates agreed on a set of demands that included the six-hour day, demands that would be made by all the branches during a statewide strike to be called at a later date that summer, when the union had established a solid base throughout Arizona and the Southwest.

Nevertheless, when Bisbee went on strike ten days later on its own initiative, the six-hour day was omitted from the union's set of demands. This led to a heated debate between the Bisbee branch and Grover Perry. The Bisbee branch even pressured the Jerome branch, which had gone on strike to support Bisbee, urging them to delete the six-hour day as a strike demand. Still, speakers at union rallies held in Bisbee raised the six-hour day as a future demand to be won once the more basic demands of the current strike were won. The two sides continued the debate the issue even after the strike was broken.

DOCUMENT EIGHT

Letter

Bisbee Executive Committee to Joseph Oates

Bisbee, Ariz. 7-6-17

Joe Oates
Miami, Ariz.

Fellow Worker:

We are informed that Jerome is out for a six hour day; this is against the decisions made during the convention; it is a well known fact that we were to organize and educate on the present demands all ready presented by Butte, Bisbee, Globe and Miami, and, when this was accomplished, we were to agitate the six hour day; this action Jerome has taken bids fair to wreck havoc to this organization throughout the whole Metal Mining Industry.

We, the Executive Committee of Bisbee Metal Mine Workers Union No. 800 go on record as opposed to this action taken by Jerome, and we further more suggest that you take the same action on this matter as we have.

We are sending M.C. Sullivan of our Executive Committee to Jerome to try and repair damage already done. We suggest that this be explained to the public that the action taken by Jerome was a misunderstanding of decisions made during Convention held here.

We appeal to you for your assistance in straightening this matter out, if possible.

Executive Committee
Bisbee Metal Mine Workers Union No. 800

IWW Trial Transcript, pp. 9134-35

DOCUMENT NINE

Letter

Grover Perry to the Bisbee Executive Committee

July 10, 1917

Executive Committee
Box 2386
Bisbee, Ariz.

Fellow Workers:

I have your letter of July 6th and content of same have been carefully noted by me, as well as fellow workers O'Hair and MacKinnon.[21] My understanding of the proceedings of the convention in Bisbee is that it was to discourage all local strikes, and agitate for a universal, or at least a statewide strike, and that the demands passed upon by the convention were to be the uniform demands presented at that strike.[22] There was nothing said in the convention that we should make the demands that were being made in Butte. Bisbee was the first to go, and although we considered that it would have been better if they had waited a few weeks, still we realize that, as long as the move had been made, we should attempt to make it universal, or at least statewide. Globe, Miami, Jerome, Golconda, and other Arizona strikes were called because Bisbee had first decided the move. I was very glad to see that Jerome, at least, came out flat-footed for the six hour day.

In conversations over the telephone with Fellow Worker Embree, he assured me that it would only be a matter of a day or so when Bisbee would incorporate the six hour day in their demands also. He further assured both Fellow Worker O'Hair and myself that if Globe, Miami, or any other camp was to take the initiative in asking for the six hour day, that Bisbee would be in line.

There is no time like the present to demand the six hour day in all mining camps. The Bisbee demands mean nothing in most mining camps, if we leave the six hour day program out. The physical examination prevails only in Bisbee and Oatman. Two men still work on all machines in Utah and in may other places. The sliding-scale does not prevail in any but Arizona camps, and in [only a] few Arizona camps. The wages of six dollars per shift for underground men is scarcely more than they would receive during the month of July under the sliding-scale.

The six hour day is the real move and it was the six hour day rallying cry in Globe, Miami, Jerome, Golconda, and elsewhere that made the great statewide strike in Arizona possible. It is the six hour day program that is going to make possible camps in Utah going out. Also, it is the six hour day program that is going to prove the greatest factor in swinging men from the W.F.M. into the I.W.W.

The first communication that I received relative to the Butte strike was a telegram which was read at the convention, and heartily applauded by all delegates, and which read as follows: Thousands of miners in Butte on strike. Now is the time for Arizona to cooperate with us for the six hour day.[23]

I note that you have sent fellow worker Sullivan to Jerome and hope that he will be able to do good work there in lining up men into the One Big Union, but sincerely hope and trust that he will not shatter the splendid determination of the men there to stand up for the six hour day program. I trust that the next communication received from Bisbee will be news from Bisbee [that it] too has decided to go out for the six hour day.

With Best Wishes, I am
Yours for Industrial Freedom,
Secretary-Treasurer

IWW Trial Transcript, pp. 8115-18

The Bisbee Deportation

For two weeks, the Bisbee branch of the Metal Mine Workers' Industrial Union #800 sustained an effective strike of thousands of miners. In the midst of a wartime emergency, the production of a vital commodity, copper, was sharply curtailed. Bisbee's city officials, working in collusion with the mining companies, instituted a series of provocative actions hoping to break the solidarity and morale of the strikers, but the miners remained united and defiant. Union leaders maintained a tight discipline on the picket lines and bars were closed for the duration of the strike.

In the early hours of July 12, 1917, hundreds of armed vigilantes, backed by machine guns provided by the mining companies, began rounding up two thousand striking miners. They were forcibly marched several miles to a railroad terminus, where they were confined to a bullpen for several hours in the baking sun of an Arizona summer day. Twelve hundred strikers were then packed into cattle cars and dumped in the desert. Hundreds more were deported from Bisbee during the following days. Vigilantes patrolled the streets for several months after the deportation, making sure that no strikers were able to return to their homes. The IWW was crushed by force in Bisbee.

The Bisbee deportation was a critical moment in IWW history. Needless to say, government prosecutors had no desire to focus on these events, so few documents from the IWW's correspondence covering these dramatic events were introduced as evidence during the Chicago trial. At the time, the union sent a few of the deported miners around the country raising funds and describing the course of the strike from the point of view of the IWW.

The following report was written by the leaders of the strike nine days after the deportation, and printed in *Solidarity* shortly afterward. At the time, the deported strikers were being held in a federal detention center in Columbus, New Mexico. They were released several weeks later. Prevented from returning to Bisbee, they scattered across the Western states.

DOCUMENT TEN

Article

Bisbee Branch Press Committee

Solidarity

July 28, 1917

July 12, 1917 is the day that we will remember for a lifetime. The master class, beaten at their own game of law and order, lost no time in using other methods which suited them better. The mines of Bisbee were practically shut down; the mine owners of Wall Street were losing thousands and thousands of dollars daily and hourly. Parts of the mines were caving in, but rather than grant the workers their modest and just demands, they resorted to mob rule. The happenings of the last few days have been of great educational value not only to the 4500 striking miners of Bisbee, but to slaves all over the world.

Small business men, inflamed by the local kept press and the corporations' howls, and, of course, as they considered their economic interest to be with the masters instead of with the advancing proletariat, they lined up against the miners. Also, the broken-down faithful slaves who had been scabbing lined up at the crack of the whip with bankers, lawyers, and high-salaried managers. Of course, all the white-collared slaves were in the "law and order" bunch of self-styled "patriotic citizens."

These were the people who did the masters' dirty work. Business men from Tombstone and Douglas came into Bisbee in the small hours of the morning, altogether forming a posse of 1200. They were deputized by the servile sheriff, who was determined to serve his master well. Some were deputized by telephone; they wore white handkerchiefs around their arms. Many wore big tin stars, of which they were very proud. Most all of them had either six-shooters or automatic pistols, and also carried a high-power rifle or a riot pump gun.

This deputized mob representing "law and order" started out about 5 am on their campaign of terrorism and anarchy. They rounded up men of every description, as they appeared on the street one by one. Not satisfied with that, gangs of 20 and 30 commenced to raid and ransack private houses. They dragged married men from their beds. One man was dragged from his wife, who bore a child two hours after he was deported. Many women were beaten and insulted. Money and clothes were openly stolen. We learned a great lesson in "law and order." Two restaurants were closed by order of the Sheriff's legal mob; the proprietors, cooks, waiters and dishwashers were driven to the cattle car at rifle point. A prominent lawyer was also corralled, and anyone who openly sympathized with the miners or showed any tendency of being a thinking human being was rounded up and herded to the Port Office square, which was surrounded by hundreds of the vigilantes, many of whom were nervous YMCA boys, who kept their fingers on the triggers, while their knees were shaking.

The miners were taken altogether by surprise, and not being armed, took the situation philosophically. We had been peaceful and orderly since the beginning of the strike. They had instilled the doctrine of law and order into us night and day. But we were disillusioned on that memorable day, July 12th. The sight of those human hounds with rifles leveled taught us a lesson long to be remembered by the working class. The corporations, beaten and on their last legs, threw off the mask of respectability and assumed their true character of murderous thugs. Several women are badly beaten, and many of the men have cut and bruised heads. Two were killed, a gunman and a fellow worker.[24] The Fellow Worker's name was Brew; he worked at the Dean mine before the strike.

After they had enough of us together, we marched down the canyon to Warren, lined on each side with the scaly snakes. We then were herded into the ball park at Warren, and then we started to cheer. This was probably one of the greatest exhibitions of solidarity ever shown. Fellow Workers made speeches in Spanish and English amidst the roaring cheers. The air with blue with curses, and we swore to stick together whatever might happen. Guns were aimed at the workers; women and young and old were shouting defiance at the human monsters who were breaking up their homes. It seemed for a few minutes as if the social revolution was on. We were defenseless, but our spirit was unbroken.

Another bunch was marched into the park amidst deafening hurrahs. We relied with wild cheers; hats went up in the air, and the thousand deputies again leveled their guns. A never dying working class solidarity there and then formed in all our hearts. We had learned that the master class only uses law and order methods when that suits them best.

The Sheriff of Cochise County upon whom the responsibility for the whole affair fell, sent unarmed men over to our side of the park to parley with us. They announced that any of us who would go back to work would be released. In answer to the question, an ear-splitting chorus of "No" was heard for minutes. Our solidarity was complete; only three or four weakened out of thirteen hundred. After a few hours, a train of 24 cars, mostly box cars and a few cattle cars, backed up the hill from Douglas. We formed in bunches of about fifty, and were loaded into these, cheering and singing "Hold the Fort."

Many of the men had lived in Bisbee for years, had wives and children; many had property and money in the bank. But in this mad frenzy of "law and order," all were loaded in the hot and filthy box cars. About 600 gunmen got on the top, and the union scabs hauled the train away.

We passed through Douglas, where a number of vigilantes were on hand with more rifles to guard against our getting off the train. All telegraph and telephone service was censored. The manager of the Western Union Telegraph Co. said afterward that he thought that it was an army captain who ordered him not to send any messages relating to the wholesale deportation. It turned out that the person who played censor was the manager of the Copper Queen smelter in Douglas, and, when questioned, he said that he was acting on authority of the Sheriff. The Sheriff, who was elected "as the working man's friend" tried to shift the blame on someone else; he was one of those who "captured" the union hall.

The day before the raid, the Mayor of Bisbee, who is a foreman in the employ of the C & A Co. said that he hoped we would lose, and he issued orders denying us the use of the City Park.[25] The propaganda of the One Big Union was (and is) spreading like wildfire throughout Arizona; the workers were beginning to wonder why the copper barons should enjoy all the good things of life, while the workers who produce everything were not even given a decent living. The corporations were desperate; the slaves were getting wise. Little did the masters know that their inhuman treatment of us and our wives would help the cause, and be the means of issuing hundreds more red cards to the now awakened slaves, who realize that their only hope is to organize, and organize right in the One Big Union.

The train rolled on until we reached Columbus, N.M., 174 miles from Bisbee. There the vigilantes left us, and went up town; they thought that we would scatter to the mesquite and disband; they did not take into consideration the fact that we were organized. We remained in the cars, and pretty soon the gunmen came back. The authorities in Columbus had arrested the head gunman and the railroad superintendent who was in charge of our train for bringing us forcibly into Columbus in defiance of all law. They told the other gunmen to leave town immediately, and take the train back with them. So the engine coupled on the tail and started back west again. At Hermanos, the gunmen left, and caught a train back to Bisbee. We, with 24 hot cars, were ditched there in the desert. No water and no food, [so] there was much suffering amongst us. Hermanos had a population of about ten people, besides a company of soldiers stationed there. The soldiers only had enough provisions on hand for themselves, and so could not help us. We laid out in the hot desert sun all the next day, Friday, with nothing to eat. The soldiers furnished us with plenty of water, and, by evening, a car of provisions came from the government Quartermaster Corps at El Paso. There was no one to "guard" us all the time we were on the desert at Hermanos, but only a very few men left out of the whole bunch. We were determined to stick together. No one was forced to stay, but we all agreed to stick together. We had speeches and singing, and cries of "Viva la Huelga" came from our Mexican Fellow Workers.

Next morning, a troop of soldiers came from Douglas, and they coupled on our box cars, and we came into Columbus again. Here the federal government took us in charge, and we pitched tents in the refugee camp. We are now here awaiting further orders. Up to this date, the vigilantes are still active in and around Bisbee in defiance of law and our constitutional rights. Governor Campbell has appealed for federal troops in Bisbee, as all the state troops are in government service.

Aftermath

The IWW vitriolically condemned the deportation and the failure of the federal government to protect the basic rights of the strikers. It sarcastically compared President Wilson's denunciations of German atrocities with his silence on the Bisbee deportation.

Refusing to Scab.

STRIKE UNBROKEN — MINERS MORE DETERMINED TO WIN THAN EVER

DEPORTED BELGIANS— AUTOCRACY

DEPORTED UNION MINERS— DEMOCRACY?

It's So Different in America!

"Refusing to Scab"

Ralph Chaplin, *Solidarity*, July 28, 1917

Still, the IWW had to do more than issue condemnations. Haywood desperately sought to extend the strike beyond Arizona, in particular to the iron ore mines of the Mesabi Range in northern Minnesota and the Upper Peninsula of Michigan. His efforts failed.

DOCUMENT ELEVEN

Letter

William Haywood to Charles Jacobson

July 26th, 1917

Chas. Jacobson
22 Lake St.
Duluth, Minnesota
Union 490

Fellow Worker:

The miners of Arizona and Butte, Montana are asking what the Minnesota miners are going to do to assist them in winning the strike.

I see where the miners of the Gogebic range in Michigan are out. Will it be possible to make it a general strike of the miners for a six hour day, six dollars a day?

Attorney Fred H. Moore briefly informed me of what you were coming to Chicago for. As you did not come, I have been expecting action on the part of the miners ever since.

With Best Wishes, I am
Yours for Industrial Freedom,
General Secretary-Treasurer

IWW Trial Transcript, p. 12236

The Bisbee strike ended in a total and decisive defeat of the union, but in the Globe-Miami district, the outcome was less dramatic. The MMWIU attempted to maintain the strike after the arrival of federal troops, but eventually the strike was lost as soldiers harassed IWW militants and provided an armed escort for strikebreakers.

The following report by one of the leading Wobblies in Arizona provides a contemporary description of the Bisbee deportation and the harsh repression that characterized the military occupation of the Globe-Miami district. The bitterness expressed in this report reflects the general sense of defeat and demoralization that ensued after the quashing of the Arizona miners' strikes and stands in sharp contrast with the euphoria felt during the first days of the strike.

DOCUMENT TWELVE

Circular

R.J. Bobba

Fellow Workers:

We are calling on you in this hour of distress.

The miners of Arizona who produce the bulk of the copper of the United States have been driven to the strike as a weapon to enforce our demands for human conditions and better pay that will in a measure meet the ever increasing cost of living. Despite our efforts to conduct the strike in strict conformity to law and order, we have been surrounded by GUNMEN in the pay of the copper companies; these gunmen are backed by the Loyalty League who, under the plea of patriotism, are giving their sanction to the most brutal methods known in the barbaric age.

Two thousand of our fellow workers in Bisbee, Arizona have been herded together by a broadcloth mob, armed with rifles and machine guns; these men have been loaded into box cars as so many swine, hauled into the desert of New Mexico without food or water, and left to starve.

The wives of some of our fellow workers of Bisbee have been beaten by gunmen, and several have been murdered. Here in this district, we have suffered all the humiliations that can be heaped upon us at the hands of the copper barons. Three score of our fellow workers have been arrested upon trumped up charges, and are now facing a capitalist court as a hope of escaping the penitentiary. A decree has gone forth from the Loyalty League that we of the [Metal] Mine Workers' Industrial Union must be EXTERMINATED. We are 100% strong in this district, and will not be deported. To the principals of solidarity we have dedicated our lives, and our stay in this district shall be as eternal as the hills from which we dig the ore. Not an ounce of copper has come to the surface since the strike was called, and we will never give up the struggle.

THE METAL MINE WORKERS' INDUSTRIAL UNION No. 800 calls YOU through this defense committee to assist us with a cash contribution for the defense of our fellow workers. The need is urgent, and the cause is the cause of all humanity. ACT AT ONCE.

Mail your remittance to R.J. Bobba, P.O. Box 1874, Miami, Arizona.

        YOURS FOR INDUSTRIAL FREEDOM,
        R.J. Bobba
        Sec.-Treas. Defense Committee

IWW Trial Transcript, pp. 9412-4

The Lumberjack Strike of 1917

Throughout the Pacific Northwest, the timber industry was a major source of employment, with thousands employed as lumberjacks in timber camps scattered throughout the region. Lumberjacks had to bring their own bedding and were fed cheap, poor quality food and housed in crowded and unsanitary dormitories. Although the work was physically demanding and dangerous, essential safety precautions were frequently ignored.

Many lumberjacks were single men, who traveled from camp to camp for most of the year, spending the winter in nearby cities such as Portland, Seattle, or Spokane. Other lumberjacks owned small, unproductive farms and worked in the timber industry part of the year to supplement their income.

Most of the region's forests were owned by powerful corporations controlled by Eastern capitalists, such as the Rockefeller family. The timber companies were determined that wages would remain low and that their workforce would not be represented by a union.

Although the IWW had been unable to successfully organize the lumberjacks of the Pacific Northwest during its first decade of existence, the situation changed dramatically as a result of the economic boom generated by World War I. (An earlier drive to organize lumberjacks in the forests of Louisiana and eastern Texas had been crushed in 1913.) During the fall of 1916, the Agricultural Workers' Industrial Union #400 began funding organizers to travel to the many small logging communities throughout the Pacific Northwest. They found a receptive audience, as thousands of timber workers joined the IWW.

Soon, the Agricultural Workers' Union had enrolled a significant number of lumberjacks within its ranks. The IWW's General Executive Board, at Haywood's urging, insisted that the AWIU limit its jurisdiction to migrant agricultural workers, so a new industrial union was chartered. The new union, the Lumber Workers' Industrial Union #500, held its founding conference in Spokane in March 1917. Delegates voted to organize a strike of the entire Pacific Northwest timber industry to begin that summer, and chose James Rowan to be the secretary of the new union.

Rowan was born in 1878 in Ireland. He immigrated to the United States in 1897, working at various jobs in the New England region. In 1911, Rowan moved to the Pacific Northwest and began working as a lumberjack. He joined the IWW in 1912 and quickly rose in prominence. Rowan was sent to Everett, Washington, in August 1916, during a free speech dispute that was sparked by IWW support of a strike of shingle weavers. While arrested, Rowan was brutally beaten by sheriff's deputies. In early 1917, he was touring timber camps as an organizer when the founding conference of the Lumber Workers' Union elected him as its secretary. Rowan was a popular figure, becoming known as the 'Jesus of the Lumberjacks.'

The timber industry of the Pacific Northwest extended from northern Montana along the Canadian border to the Pacific Ocean and then down along the coast into Oregon. The IWW found the most success in organizing the lumberjacks of northern Idaho and northwest Montana, where the union provided a welcoming community for workers who spent months in small, isolated communities. The Lumber Workers' Industrial Union understood this, and thus located its headquarters in Spokane, Washington, the closest city to that area.

In mid-April 1917, spontaneous strikes were initiated in isolated timber camps in northwestern Montana and northern Idaho. These strikes soon spread throughout the forests of Montana, Idaho and eastern Washington and then into the forests west of the Cascade Mountains in western Washington and along the Oregon coast. From the start, the federal government sent troops to disperse picket lines and escort strikebreakers into timber camps.

By June 1917, the strike had spread so widely that the union decided to make it a general strike of lumberjacks throughout the Northwest. The federal government responded by ratcheting up its repressive tactics. Wobblies were pulled off trains and arrested. Hundreds of IWW activists were detained without charges by the military and many were held for weeks in makeshift bullpens. Union halls were raided and shut down as the Wilson administration made it clear that it was intent on suppressing the strike.

Rowan responded by calling a general strike of all IWW unions in the Pacific Northwest to begin on August 20, 1917, demanding an end to government repression. This was particularly intended to widen the strike to include migrant agricultural workers. On the eve of the strike, Rowan and two dozen other strike leaders were detained by the military. The general strike fizzled and, soon afterward, the Lumber Workers' Union brought the strike of lumberjacks to an end. Instead, the union resorted to creative tactics of disruption, as lumberjacks came to timber camps without their own bedding, in an effort to force the companies to provide it. Wobbly lumberjacks also tried to establish an eight hour day in specific camps by quitting work after eight hours on the job.

In the end, the improvised job actions faded away. Conditions in timber camps in the Pacific Northwest improved, with better housing and more nutritious food being furnished, but the ten-hour day remained the norm. Although the effort to build a militant union of lumberjacks had been quashed, the IWW still retained a considerable base of support. In the early 1920s, one day general strikes were called to demand the release of Wobbly political prisoners. Only after 1924, in the aftermath of a disastrous internal split, did the IWW cease to act as a significant force in the timber camps of the Pacific Northwest.

The Strike Spreads

The initial plan for the strike, as determined by the delegates at the founding convention of the Lumber Workers' Union in March 1917, was to slowly build up momentum through local strikes, only organizing a general strike of the entire Pacific Northwest timber industry in the summer of 1917. Instead, the militancy of the rank and file forced the pace of the strike.

Soon after the founding conference was held, the rivers crossing the forests of northwestern Montana and northern Idaho began thawing. Logs that had been felled the previous autumn, just before the winter snows set in, were floated down rivers to sawmills for processing. (Timber camps were located in isolated, mountainous areas where no roads existed.) The union began calling impromptu, local strikes of river men, the skilled workers who steered the logs downstream, and the strike had begun.

DOCUMENT ONE

Letter

Don Sheridan to William Haywood

April 30, 1917

William D. Haywood
Fellow Worker:

Your letters of the 25th and 27th at hand and carefully read. Note the supplies have been sent to Duluth as per order.

Have letter from Clarence Edwards in Alexandria[1] today. He gives some news about the conditions there, but is of the opinion that it will be a hard job to organize the loggers and lumber workers again.

I have not received the song books yet. Do you know if they have been shipped? I have ordered some from Minneapolis, as I am out entirely.

The strike situation here: conditions favorable to the striker. Turner, Miller and the strike committee were all arrested, but are now out on bail. They are to be tried today. They were arrested as the result of a frame up between the mayor of Eureka[2] and the sup't of the company. Their plan was heard over the phone, and they were ridiculed by the citizens. We are confident that they will be turned loose. The strikers are behaving fine; there has been no rioting or disorder of any kind, and the sentiment of the entire community is with the strikers. I think it will be settled in a couple of weeks at most. The other drives are just coming out, and we will have our hands full for some time, as we are determined to make them pay the scale we have set. As you are aware, the St. Maries strikers won out on all of their demands, and donated a day's pay to the Fortine bunch.[3] We still need the money as it costs like the dickens. I am enclosing financial reports, so you will see how #500 stands.

Everything is going along fairly well here, but the war situation is raising the mischief with us. They are just aching for a chance to turn loose on us, and yet I hardly think they dare do it either.

With Best Wishes, I am
Yours for Industrial Freedom
Sec'y Spokane District I.W.W.

IWW Trial Transcript, pp. 11265-66

The Strike at Its Zenith

As the snowdrifts of winter disappeared, more timber camps reopened and the strike spread. The Lumber Workers' Union worked hard to avoid violent confrontations with the authorities, while urging lumberjacks to avoid disorderly conduct in local communities. With the strike gaining momentum, strike leaders became more confident of victory.

DOCUMENT TWO

Letter

Joseph Ratti to James Rowan

Whitefish, Mont.
5/22/17

James Rowan
Fellow Worker:

Just received 600 dues stamps and check for $200.00, [and am] in good shape. Yesterday and today sent a big bunch of supplies and such to the Wyack Camp on the Flathead [River]. The men there are in good spirits, and determined, $5.00 for 8 hours, or no driving. The men on the Stillwater [River] are also doing good.[4] No dissension and no talking compromise. Anyone talking compromise is either a stool pigeon, or a weakling, at this stage of the game. The hall was opened yesterday in Kalispell,[5] and it will undoubtedly do good work. But don't you think that putting a hall in every little town, that the expense will be enormous, and with this strike on too. Of course, you know more about things like that than I, but, you know, too many hands spoil the stew, meaning that you have no home industries in Kalispell, or here. We are depending on the lumber camps, and they are pretty well organized, and a hall there, and one here, would not stop up for keeps, of course. I am satisfied with anything that is done, but I am entitled to my opinion. Things around here are getting dead on account of this strike; men will not come through the strike zone, but we are plugging on, slow and sure. Boosting for the O.B.U.

> I am for Emancipation,
> Jos. J. Ratti, Del. 5

P.S. What in hell are we going to do about registration? Do the one year, eh?

IWW Trial Transcript, pp. 12674-75

DOCUMENT THREE

Letter

James Rowan to Joseph Ratti

May 24, 1917

Jos. J. Ratti
Whitefish, Mont.

Fellow Worker:

Your letter of the 22nd at hand and contents noted. I see that you are getting the chuck out to the boys, and that will make them feel pretty good; as long as their stomachs are well filled they will put up a good scrap. Note about your comment on the hall at Kalispell, and, while it may be quite an expense, yet the establishment of these halls at the central point gives the organization a prestige and an appearance of permanency that is worth a great deal. Of course, if we find that the maintenance of all these halls is too costly, we will have to close some of them up, but I hardly think that they are too close together yet. There are always a bunch of natives that you can get by having a permanent place for them to congregate, and we must get all the workers in the O.B.U.

Regarding the conscription law, will say that the boys have decided to ignore it. That, we understand, is also what they are going to do on the coast. Of course, we are not taking any official stand on the matter, as the General Organization has said nothing about the matter so far. May receive some communication on this later.

Yours for Industrial Freedom,
Sec'y Industrial Union #500, I.W.W.

IWW Trial Transcript, pp. 12675-6

The Demands of the Lumberjacks

Since the Lumber Workers' Union emerged out of the Agricultural Workers' Union, the initial demands raised by the strikers had been formulated by Walter Nef, the secretary of the AWIU, who was not familiar with the specific grievances of lumberjacks. As the strike unfolded, the union clarified its list of demands. The eight-hour day is listed as the first demand because this was an issue that unified all of the strikers. It became the central demand of the strike. Another crucial demand called for most new hires to be made through union halls.

DOCUMENT FOUR

Letter

Richard Brazier to J.A. Macdonald

8/6/[17]

J.A. Macdonald
Editor, *Industrial Worker*
Seattle, Wash.

Fellow Worker;

Please find enclosed herewith M.O. For $3.00 in payment for B.O. #6.

Also, find enclosed revised demands for the Lumber Workers. The last demands printed in the Worker were not considered strong enough by the men on the job, as some camps were already paying the $3.00 we were asking for, and those camps not paying the $3.00 would be paying it anyway in the near future. So, we have decided to ask for the flat increase of 50 cents per day, and the 20 per cent increase for the men paid by the month, like the teamsters, with the $3.00 [to] still be the minimum. Also, we decided that the 8 hour day would just as well be fought for now, as any other time. Also, make the introduction of the clause for overtime, that is time and a half, and double time for Sundays and holidays. This measure is a punitive measure to prevent overtime, but, as all overtime at this stage of the game cannot be prevented, we are trying to see that whatever overtime [that] is worked shall be paid for extra.

Also, we introduced the demand to abolish the carrying of blankets by demanding the companies furnish mattresses and bedding. All in all, the men on the job think these demands will meet with more approval than the previous demands sent in by Nef.

Also, note the demand for the reduction of board that should meet with popular approval amongst the lumberjacks.

Also, note the demand for the abolition of hiring men through the employment agencies has been amplified.

Hoping you will find the space to print these demands as soon as you possibly can in order that we may start as soon as we possibly can to circulate the demands amongst the camps.

I remain yours for the O.B.U.,
Richard Brazier
Sec'y Spokane Branch

IWW Trial Transcript, pp. 18798-9

DOCUMENT FIVE

Enclosed: DEMANDS OF LUMBER WORKERS OF MONTANA, IDAHO, AND EASTERN WASHINGTON

[August 1917]

FIRST

To demand an eight hour day. Time and a half for overtime, double time for Sundays and holidays.

SECOND

All men employed by the day shall receive an increase in wages of 50 cents per day. All men employed by the month shall receive a 20 per cent increase of wages. There shall be a minimum of $3.00 per day, that is no man employed by the day shall receive less than $3.00 per day of eight hours.

THIRD

The charge for board shall not exceed 75 cents per day.

FOURTH

Good, clean, wholesome food; such alterations and improvements in the cookhouse as the cook may designate.

FIFTH

Good, clean place to sleep, plenty of room with no top bunks. The companies to furnish mattresses and plenty of good, clean bedding. Bunkhouses must be properly ventilated and kept clean. Extra dry house must be installed; also, shower baths and wash room, equipped with plenty of soap and clean towels.

SIXTH

No men to be hired through employment agencies. All men to be hired at the camps, or from the union halls.

SEVENTH

There shall be no discrimination against Union men.

IWW Trial Transcript, pp. 18799-18800.

Strike Tactics

Sustaining a strike involving dozens of lumber camps dotted across several states was a daunting task. Although Rowan coordinated the activities of the Lumber Workers' Union from its headquarters, most tactical decisions were made on the spot by delegates located in small towns and lumber camps hundreds of miles from Spokane.

The following correspondence reflects the frustration felt by one delegate, Charles Knights, as he attempted to shut down a small camp in northwestern Montana that was producing timber by recruiting strikebreakers. In this situation, the union often placed militants posing as strikebreakers within the camp, where they would try to stall production and persuade wavering lumberjacks to quit work. In this case, Knights was in touch with those planted inside encouraging them to engage in low-level acts of sabotage targeting one strikebreaker who had previously been an IWW member.

In general, Rowan and the Lumber Workers' Union urged strikers to eschew violence and avoid violent confrontations with security guards and police. Nevertheless, Rowan endorsed the specific plan of action being used in this case. It is hard to see how this use of sabotage could have helped to further the strike. These actions could only confuse those on strike as to the union's stance on violence, while providing the authorities with an excuse to utilize force to break the strike.

DOCUMENT SIX

Letter

James Rowan to Charles Knights

May 31, 1917

Chas Knights
Troy, Mont.

Fellow Worker:

Your letter of the 26th at hand and contents carefully read. When writing letters on the typewriter, don't forget to sign your name, as we cannot tell who they come from otherwise, unless we guess at it. Note that there are five men rolling logs off the bank at Libby. I guess you will do what you can to get them off. Also, note that you are trying to get Wallace back there, and that would be alright, as he is O.K. Note about the fellow worker tearing his card up, and when we are sure of that fact, we will make a record of it.

In your other letter, I note that Stewart and DeWolf, some name, are busy guarding against wobs in the camp; see that you have an ally in one of the deputies, and that is a good idea, of course. You will use your own judgment about how far to trust him, but use him all you can. We will not mention anything about him in the bulletin, as the information is too valuable for us to queer the source of it.

I see that the booze is worrying you some, and it is bad dope alright. You will have to get a bunch of the boys who can stay [away] from it, and let [them] take the most important places in the strike. See to it that the right men are placed in each camp, if you have more than one. There will be some drunks alright, but if there are a few whom you can depend on scattered around, you will know what is going on at least.

Will see it that you get the *Workers* alright.

With Best Wishes, I am
Yours for Industrial Freedom
Sec'y Industrial Union, #500 I.W.W.

IWW Trial Transcript, pp. 12687-8

DOCUMENT SEVEN

Letter (484)

Charles Knights to James Rowan

Troy, Mont., June 1st/17

James Rowan
Spokane, Wash.

Fellow Worker:

We have succeeded in getting one man [in] the Kootenar[6] last night, and there is a Frenchman there, and he is the only boatman on the job. There is a bunch on there [who are] old timers in the woods, but not on the rivers. They are mostly old men that can not do anything but swamp any more. We have succeeded in getting some of those handbills in the camp, and they have all had a chance to read them. We have our jungle outfit at Kootenar Falls, about [a] ¼ of a mile away from the scab camp, and [we] intend to give them guts until we get them off [the job]. From our jungle camp, it is in an out of the way place, [the] nearest saloon is [in] Troy, seven miles, or else Libby[7], eleven miles. When we pulled the Kootenar, we had a few good river drivers, but there was no booze handy, and they left. We are going to snare some more, and [we] have [the] advantage [that] all freights stop at the jungle outfit. So, we are shaking down the trains to try and get a good bunch going to them all the time.

About this guy Fisher, his name is Fred Fisher, card No. 253363, and he was a delegate to the lumberworkers' convention in Spokane. He has torn up his card, and is working on the river. They used a drayman's team in Libby to pull [move] this camp for them, and a wob is driving it. On the evening of the 29th, the skinner traded shoes with this fellow Fisher, and the skinner and the deputy had no lye, so they filled his shoes with pepper. Last night, I sent them a can of lye, and yesterday, when they moved camp, the deputy poured a half of a five gallon can of coal oil over Fisher's bed, [so] if they move again there will be no more bed.

On the afternoon of the 29th, when the pickets tried to get to the boat men, there were about seven or eight logs clean across the river. They (the camp foremen) took the boat crew across [the river], and they sat down over there for about three hours, and had nothing to do, but they did not want the men on the bank to get to them (the strikebreakers).

There are eight men working, and we think [that] we can get a complete tie up on this ditch, but the class that is on it is no good. This deputy is proving himself [the] joke in the camp. The wob skinner says he is all the time spaning [spinning] up something on the scabs. He said if we sent him up the can of Wobbly itch he would sure use it, and now he has it. Sand Bar is nuts. He doesn't know what in hell to think of us now. You see we have no place to keep our church except in the woods, and we just have to try it as we use it. I have twelve men in camp last night, but they are not all river men. Still, I think I can get a good bunch up there.

I have not heard from Wallace the last few days. He would be a lot of help here if we could get him [here] now.

I will write an article for the *Worker* and both the first of the week, so as to get them there in good time to go to press. Will keep you posted on all developments all the time. I am going to Libby today, and visit the sick man. Send all mail to Troy, as we can make pretty good train connections to camp.

Yours for a Victory in [the] Near Future,
Chas. Knights

IWW Trial Transcript, pp. 12688-90

DOCUMENT EIGHT

Letter

James Rowan to Charles Knights

June 1, 1917

Charles Knights
Troy, Mont.

Fellow Worker:

Your letter of the 1st at hand and contents carefully read. Glad to note that the cat is loose and making things interesting for the scabs.[8] It will be a good idea to keep the cat going on this strike if you can. We did not make much use on the other strikes, and it might have been better if we had used it a little more. Note that you are getting the river drivers off the trains, and you will no doubt be able to scare up a good bunch. See about Fred Fisher tearing up his card, and we will make a record of it. Wallace is around there somewhere, and you ought to be able to get in touch with him. Note that you are going to keep us posted, and that is what we want.

> With best wishes, I am
> Yours for Industrial Freedom,
> Sec'y Industrial Union, #500 I.W.W.

IWW Trial transcript, P. 12691

In a few cases, local strikes were so effective in cutting production that the boss in a camp was prepared to sign a contract conceding the demands of the lumberjacks if the union agreed to not call any strikes during the duration of the timber season. Such a contract would have violated the IWW Constitution, which prohibited agreements that precluded strikes during the length of the contract. The IWW emphasized the necessity of class solidarity and it was therefore concerned that acceptance of such contracts would inhibit solidarity strikes.

When Rowan was queried by a delegate on this issue, he reiterated the union's general perspective while suggesting that, if necessary, a branch could sign such an agreement, but would not be bound by it. Ultimately, the union decided that it would be a tactical mistake to sign contracts with a few isolated timber camps when it was seeking to spread the strike throughout the Pacific Northwest in an effort to gain an agreement that would cover all of the timber camps in the region.

DOCUMENT NINE
Letter
James Rowan to D.B. Ward

Spokane, Wash., June 13, 1917

D.B. Ward
Odessa, Wash.

Fellow Worker:

Your letter of the 11th at hand and contents noted. Enclosed you will find M.O. for $25.00. Let us know if you need any more as [we] will only send you money in small amounts as many of our delegates and sec'y get arrested when [they] have money, and it is lost or tied up. Note that the contractor would come through with all the demands provided you sign the contract not to give any further trouble while the job lasts. Well, contracts are not sacred, and if you have to sign it, you can do it. You can always break a contract, you know. However, it may be best to try and win out the way you are trying to. Note that there have been no scabs on the job since you went on strike, and that sounds as though you will win out in [a] short time. Let us know how you are getting on.

With Best Wishes, I am
Yours for Industrial Freedom
James Rowan
Sec'y Spokane District, A.W.O.

P.S.: It is like this Ward, we don't give a damn for contracts. What we are after is the wages and hours and conditions. We never waste any energy trying to make the boss sign an agreement to hire all men from the union hall, because he would only break it if he had the power. And, if we have the power to make him hire all wobblies, we don't need a contract for we will make him do it anyway.

IWW Trial Transcript, pp. 12719-20

By June 1917, the strike had spread through several states and was rapidly gaining momentum. Rank and file lumberjacks were urging the union to call everyone out instead of relying on a series of localized actions. At the same time, Army soldiers were being deployed throughout the region to quell local strikes by escorting strikebreakers across picket lines.

The following letter indicates Rowan's awareness of this situation, as well as his reluctance to move toward a total confrontation with the timber companies. Still, the call for a general strike of the Pacific Northwest timber industry would be issued soon after this letter was written.

DOCUMENT TEN

Letter

James Rowan to John Martin

June 18, 1917

John Martin
Seattle, Wash.

Fellow Worker:
Your letter of the 16th with corrected report enclosed at hand and contents noted. Enclosed you will find the bill for the supplies that are being sent to you. We are sending the Rev. I.W.W., which was ordered some time ago, and will send the gold buttons as soon as they get more; they have been ordered for some time now. Note that you will try and avoid any mistakes, and that will help this office out greatly.

With Best Wishes, I am,
Yours for Industrial Freedom,
James Rowan

P.S. What do you think about a general strike in the lumber industry? How do you think the members on the coast would respond to a general strike call? A strike has started in the Humbird camp at Sandpoint[9], and it looks like it is going to spread. Now we figured on a general strike this summer, but not quite as soon as this. There is trouble starting in Butte. The military are getting very hostile in Montana. I see by your telegram you fellows had your share of trouble in Seattle. Let me know as soon as possible what you think of this general strike proposition. It looks like we will be forced to call as big a strike as possible very soon.

IWW Trial Transcript, p. 12757

Under Attack

Timber was a vital commodity in the war effort. Spruce trees, found in the rain forests of western Washington, were used to build airplanes. The logs produced from the forests of northwestern Montana and northern Idaho were used to prop up the maze of tunnels beneath Butte's copper mines. From the start, government troops were sent to protect strikebreakers and harass Wobbly militants. As the strike spread, the administration of Woodrow Wilson began to view it as a serious threat that had to be met with a coordinated set of repressive measures. IWW halls were raided and closed, federal troops occupied logging communities and hundreds of IWW members were detained for weeks by the military without any criminal charges being filed.

Unlike the copper industry, the timber industry was not centralized in a few localities. As the authorities crushed the strike in one timber camp, it spread to another one. The federal government responded by further ratcheting up the level of repression, using even harsher measures to intimidate the strikers.

Strike leaders could see that the balance of forces was shifting toward the employers. The following public statement by Rowan provides both a defense of the strike and a listing of the actions taken by authorities to intimidate the lumberjacks and force a return to work. Under the bravado is the awareness that the union was being pushed to its limit.

DOCUMENT ELEVEN
Declaration
James Rowan
[July 1917]

Fellow Workers:

The long suffering and submissive slaves in the lumber industry have at last risen from their groveling position in the dust, and, in justice to themselves and their class, are standing erect in class conscious revolt and defiance. He who braves the frost and flood and forest, and grapples with the primitive elements, has at last rebelled with the virulent and red-blooded manhood that his sturdy environment has worked into his being.

Just as the rude winds have worked gianthood and strength into the forest he fells, so have his conditions of life developed his fiber and determination.

The abhorrence of the foul bunk houses and the wolfish biting cold of winter, the hellish heat of summer, and the bleakness of the burdened existence, have embittered him and made him keenly alive to his wrongs and the future attainment of his rights.

And he is now seen arrayed in the gaudy uniform of mackinaw and spiked boots, battling for his life with the ONLY WORTHY weapon accessible to him-the power of INDUSTRIAL ORGANIZATION.

It is one of the most vital and terrific struggles ever waged in the industrial arena of the North West. This class conflict is a death grapple between the robber and the robbed-the Master and the Slave. One of the first defensive blows struck was the strike drives; where one is required to wade the icy mountain waters, often to sleep in wet clothing, and work from ten to fourteen hours per day. This became unendurable.

The increased cost of necessary clothing-with driving shoes as high as $12.00 per pair for the meager wage of $3-culminated [in] the final climax, when, on April 12th they set aside their peavies, rolled up their "sougans," and then quit the job.[10]

Instead of disbanding and deserting the community, as experience heretofore has shown to be [in]correct and abortive, they immediately established headquarters, and put out vigilant picket lines.

The soberness, solidarity and orderliness of the strikers surprised and bitterly disappointed the "powers that be."

They had the conception and hope that the men would become drunken and disorderly, and give them the opportunity to use the civil and military forces to disrupt and defeat them.

The prostitute, lick-spittle authorities who are ever eager to hear and obey "the Master's Voice,"[11] erected a crude "bullpen,"[12] in anticipation of labor troubles; they even blatantly boasted it was especially built for the entertainment of "wobblies."

Soon, a body of about 140 soldiers arrived on the scene, supposedly to protect railroad property, but they at once were stationed along the river, and began guarding the scabs.

The military claims to have been misinformed about conditions, and say they received telegrams that red riot was drenching the streets of Eureka. Being unable to trap us in any of their legal pitfalls, or fasten any bona fide charge upon us in any way, they at last, in desperation, resorted to a "trumped up" vagrancy charge, and arrested and dragged out of their beds, Organizer J. I. Turner and Delegate Louis Miller, and, [on] the following day, three of the strike and press committee. After a two-day trial by jury that advertisingly exposed their rank, raw, rotten deals of rascality, they were nakedly exposed to open ridicule and shame. The I.W.W.s emerged victorious and clean [as] the escaped prey of the jungle beasts of capitalism. The lawyer hired by the prosecution tried to inflame the public and influence the jury against us on the pretext of our lack of patriotism in being idle, and [as] a hindrance to industry in the war crisis, and claimed our actions should inspire every loyal citizen to drive us out of town.

The surrounding community of stump ranch "scissorbills" furnished a makeshift source from which "scabs" were recruited; but their inexperienced bungling only cost their masters great expense, and themselves broken limbs, and, worst of all, the ever livid branch [branding] of SCAB.

That history repeats itself is once more certain, for the old time tactic of our ancestors in "double crossing" our red brothers was resorted to at the White Earth Indian Reservation in Minnesota. Through false claims and luring promises, they herded a band together and shipped them to the slaughter. After getting them on the job, they deducted their fares and other unexpected bills, and lariated[13] them by all possible methods. The white man's modern method of plunder has thoroughly disgusted and roiled the Indians, and there is little likelihood of them ever again being able to get any more from that source.

They tried to intimidate the strikers with threats of martial law, and federal interference, but were never able to make their "bluff" stick, or embroil the troops and the strikers. The results cannot be judged other than [as] a victory. The community has made the acquaintance of the purposes and methods of the O.B.U., and everyone stands either in friendly or fearful respect of it.

To the disgrace of "the powers that be," it must be stated that they have been more successful in satiating their lust for revenge in other places. Organizer Fred Hegge at Fortine was arrested and kept under federal guard at Whitefish for fifty-eight days. They also entered [the] headquarters at Whitefish and destroyed the charter and literature, generally wrecking the place. Being unable to frighten Secretary Joe Ratti into signing papers in agreement to be neutral, they placed him under arrest [by the] Federal Guard. Ratti's arrest was followed by that of Fellow Worker Wm. Collins. Through habeas corpus proceedings, Fellow Workers Hegge, Ratti, Collins and other members have at last been released.

The hall at Bend, Oregon was recently entered and pillaged, and even the electric bulbs destroyed.

After getting permission from the property owner for speaking purposes at Couer d'Alene, Ida., Fellow Worker Morgan was prevented by the boot-licking curs of the masters [from speaking]. "Every dog has its day," [but] they will be forced to retreat into their foul kennels where they belong.

The latest press reports give the account of [the] raiding of the headquarters at North Yakima. They boast of thirty arrests.

We recognize such statements as being exceptionally true; although most [statements] they issue about the I.W.W.s [are] none other than poisonous fabrications. We only credit the veracity of the above statements through knowing that they are in exact accordance with the tactics of "violence and disorder" they preach so rabidly against, but hypocritically and brutally practice themselves.

Two Greek fellow workers were arrested at Bovill recently, and deported to Moscow, with the horrible charge of being agitators placed against them.[14] If I remember rightly, there was once a rebel from a place called Nazareth who suffered [from] a mob hurling the same charge. From all over the country, the news is flashed of the willful and malicious interference of "law and (dis)order" [with] the rights and privileges supposed to be given and guaranteed by the Constitution.

But instead of it causing us to explode in "wild frenzy," "run amuck," or to "see red," as the "Diamond Dick" authors are wont to term it, we hitch up our suspenders another notch, settle back, pleased contentment, and crack a genuine home spun, new mown, grin of the very earliest varieties, and accept the truth of an old "saw" of the "sky pilots": "THAT ALL THINGS WORK TOGETHER FOR RIGHTEOUSNESS."[15]

We clearly recognize the evolutionary economic forces underlying our movement, and analyze aright [correctly] the power backing our organization, which means the inevitable death and annihilation of the present system, and we interpret all tyrannical opposition as the pregnant pains in the birth of the NEW.

So we rejoice when our halls are entered and pillaged, our members wantonly beaten and imprisoned, for we realize with increasing gratification that each incident is a blow in the erection of the scaffold upon which capitalism shall be executed, and the digging of the grave of its eternal oblivion.

At last the slumbering giant of labor has awakened, and rubbed the stupor from his eyes, and stands forth a veritable Samson, and is shaking the foundations of the shy locks as never before.

He who fells the forests and makes them vibrant with the echo of his ax, he whose sturdy manhood braves and rides the white foamed chargers of the drive, and furnishes the energy and skill behind the whirling belts and screaming saws, has at last become keenly conscious and rebellious toward the industrial pirate who robs him of enjoying the comforts of the warmth and shelter the products of his toil has produced. The masters riot and [live] in luxury, and even "the foxes have holes; the birds of the air have nests," but he "has not where to lay his head."[16]

So behold him. Here he stands, and he extends not a thin and trembling hand, nor mumbles a beggarly appeal, but he points with gnarled, sinewy ones to the class conflict now being waged on the bright frontiers, where the battle for bread is being waged, and, unabashed and unflinchingly, calls you to the front.

In sincere realization that our organized economic power is the greatest and only accessible weapon, and our master's greatest foe, we counsel the avoidance of any actions that may breed violence.

Remember: organization, job control, and NOT WHISKEY, lands the "solar plexus" punch. Thus, shall the ONE BIG UNION sweep onward with the impetus of evolutionary scientific POWER to the end that ALL THE WORLD SHALL BE FOR ALL THE WORKERS, and instead of industrial despotism, tyranny and wrong shall reign INDUSTRIAL DEMOCRACY, LIBERTY AND LIGHT.

> When the last wild drive is over,
> And the crew is safely camped,
> And even the uncouth rover,
> His last trail has tramped,
> May the evening fires burn cheery,
> And the mess house be well supplied
> And well earned rest bless the weary
> When life's embers at last have died
> (Poem by Olin B. Anderson)

Collect and send all possible funds at once to:

> James Rowan, Sec'y Industrial Union No. 500, I.W.W.

IWW Trial Transcript, pp. 13561-8

Calling the Strike Off

The detention of Rowan and twenty-six others on August 19, 1917 marked the effective end of the lumberjacks' strike. These arrests, following upon a long series of arrests and detentions of local delegates and rank and file militants, were the final blow, and the strike crumbled.

Don Sheridan had served as the interim acting secretary of the newly founded Lumber Workers' Industrial Union in the spring of 1917, and he resumed this position after Rowan had been seized by the military. As the following correspondence indicates, Sheridan understood the difficulties of the situation, and moved quickly to bring an end to the strike. Lumberjacks returning to work would soon begin improvising guerrilla tactics on the job, but by then Sheridan was incarcerated, one of more than a hundred Wobbly leaders indicted for violating the Espionage Act in September 1917.[17]

DOCUMENT TWELVE

Letter

Don Sheridan to William Haywood

August 26, 1917

William D. Haywood
Chicago, Ill.

Fellow Worker:

Spokane is still on the I.W.W. map, though it was a little doubtful for awhile whether we could stay here after the closing of the halls or not. It was our first intention to start up in Seattle, but this plan was changed later; so, I came back here, and we will try and get going here again.

The situation here is not so bad now. We have a couple of rooms where we are doing business. We can, and are, establishing the lines of communication again.

Most of the boys have been turned loose already. Rowan, of course, is still in jail, along with about 10 others. It is rather difficult to say what they will do with them. The writ of Haber [habeas] corpus was denied, of course, and we will now take it to the Supreme Court.[18]

The strikers were not discouraged because of the closing of the office, but are more determined to win than ever. The members of #400 and #573[19] are coming out on strike, but I have no very definite information about it, as it caused quite a bit of confusion when the arrest was made.

About 30 of our members were arrested in Pasco this morning, just for being I.W.[W]'s. Most of these were #600[20] men, and some were taken off the engines. Others are being arrested through the farming country, and in plain English, we are having a hell of a time.

All of the former bunch who were in jail in Pasco have been released. All the former bunch in Yakima have also been released. They are putting some new ones in. The Ginsburg outfit have all been released with the exception of some who are being held as alien enemies.

They are holding all men of conscription age who have not registered. They are still holding practically all of the men in Moscow. The stockades at Moscow and St. Marie, Idaho are so full that they have to turn some of the prisoners loose to make room for the new ones. We are going to fill them up right and see how many more they are going to build. Nearly all of the prisoners in Idaho are charged with the "criminal syndicalism" law.[21] We will find out what it means this fall. We will have James Wallace, the attorney from Missourian, handle the cases. We will also try and secure the service of Vanderbilt as associate counsel in these cases. I think you will appreciate the importance of defeating this law. It is a matter that affects the whole organization. Any suggestion or cooperation from headquarters will be greatly appreciated.

Owing to the condition of affairs in this district at the present time, I think that the presence of a G.E.B. member would be a benefit to the organization. If one can be spared, we would welcome his suggestions.

I am acting as sec'y for the time being, but little can be done except to answer letters and do a little temporary bookkeeping etc. All the books and fixtures are in the hands of the authorities, and so nothing can be done till we get hold of them again in the way of fixing up accounts, etc. The money in the bank has been released, and we are now able to get mail, so we will be able to go ahead and keep the picket lines going.

I will keep you informed of any fresh developments, and, in the meantime, we will do the best we can.

>With Best Wishes, I am Yours for Industrial Freedom
>Don Sheridan

IWW Trial Transcript, p. 13239

DOCUMENT THIRTEEN

Letter

Don Sheridan to Earl Osborne

Spokane, Wash.
Box 2217
August 29, 1917

Earl Osborne
Tacoma, Wash.

Fellow Worker:

Your letter received and carefully read. I note that the funds are getting low; I see this by Martin's report. It is evident that some action will have to be taken, and we are of the opinion here that it would be better to have them go back to work before the strike dribbles away to nothing. We are getting low here too; in fact, there is nothing left in the treasury of #500. Some of the branches have put up the proposition of going back to work already, and it is, in my estimation, the most sensible thing that can be done.

I am informed that two of the branches, or rather strike camps, are going to send in a resolution asking for a referendum on whether the strike shall be called off or not, and you know that if they take this action that it will mean that the strike will be off. Of course, you realize that the strike can not be called off by the Organization Committee. It was started by the members, and the members will have to call it off.

There are several things to be considered in this proposition. There are the men in the jails who have to be considered, but there seems to be nothing to be gained by holding out till the strike becomes a fizzle, right? We can call it off, and go back to work, and still maintain our organization and the chances for a comeback are good. Strikes in the future will have to be I.W.W. strikes, not A.F. of L. strikes, [that is strikes] such as this one has been. We will have to put forth strenuous efforts to educate the membership before another one is attempted.

From the tone of your letter, I think that you will be in favor of calling it off. At any rate, let us hear what you think can be done in the Seattle district. Most of the membership will, I am sure, favor such a move. There will be some who will want to fight it out to the bitter end. While I might feel that way myself, I am afraid that it would mean the union would drop to nothing. By going back while we still have a strong membership, we would still have practical control in many camps, and would have a good nucleus to build from.

If you will take this matter up with Martin and the district Org. Comm., and let us know what decision you reach, we will then be able to act to get [a] united action on this. It will be better to keep this quiet till a decision is reached. I may mention that they are still jailing men here, and as it was started to defend them in the courts, we still have to go through with it.

Yours for Industrial Solidarity,
Don Sheridan, Roy A. Brown, J. Turner[22]

IWW Trial Transcript, pp. 13242-3

An Assessment

The coordinated attack launched by the federal government in the fall of 1917 had a crippling impact on the IWW. With local halls repeatedly raided, newspapers suppressed, hundreds of Wobblies in jail, and the leadership under indictment for violating the Espionage Act, the union began to unravel. The impact of government repression could even be felt in the isolated timber camps of the Pacific Northwest, as the membership of the Lumber Workers' Union plummeted, the strike was called off, and lumberjacks were forced to conceal their union ties if they wanted to find a job.

The following letter was written by James Rowan from his jail cell in Chicago as he awaited trial in federal court with dozens of other IWW leaders. By January 1918, the impact of the federal government's assault on the IWW had already become clear. Still, Rowan continued to insist that the lumberjacks would inevitably emerge victorious. In fact, there were no easy answers to the IWW's dilemma. As the union became more successful, it drew the intensive interest of the repressive agencies of the federal government. Nevertheless, a necessary first step in developing an effective response to the government's campaign of intimidation was a realistic assessment of the situation. Rowan was unable to do this.

DOCUMENT FOURTEEN

Letter[23]

James Rowan to John Grave

Cook Co. Jail
Chicago, Ill.
Jan. 10th, 1918

John Grave,

Fellow Worker:

I see your name and address in the Worker, so will drop you a line to let you know how things are at this winter health resort. There are quite a bunch of us here, and the conditions are fairly rotten, but in spite of all the drawbacks, the bunch all seem to be enjoying their vacations pretty well. It is sure interesting to meet the boys from all the different places of the country, and hear how the movement is going ahead in the different sections. The boys from the West compare favorably with the rest, and it seems they have a better understanding of the movement. The spittoon philosopher element and the anarchists seem to be pretty numerous in the East.

Well John, we sure gave the lumber trust a walloping last summer. That was the first time they were ever whipped, and they were whipped to a finish. The lumberjacks are lining up to beat hell. Last month over thirteen hundred joined. It looks like we will soon control the lumber industry. They are still fighting us in desperation, but we have got a stranglehold on them, and their case is hopeless. Of course, we expect nothing else than to be jailed after taking part in a strike like that for we know that a rebellious slave is the worst criminal in the eyes of the masters, but what the hell of it. When we understand the Redbeard philosophy[24], as you and I do, we only laugh at an old sissified can like this. It is [a] pretty feeble institution to try to break up a strong job organization with. It shows how feeble are the minds of the rulers, and how little they grasp the significance of this movement. What do you think of the Bolshevik? What they do in Russia we can do in this "Land of the Free."

Well John, I hope to hear from you soon.

Will cut her short now as I am not sure whether you will get this or not. I know you fellows have troubles of your own down there. None of the Edmonton fellows have arrived here yet, but we expect Jim Manning any time. The other Manning was turned loosed today. Also, expect Turner in near future.

With Best Wishes,
Yours for the One Big Union
James Rowan

Frank Little

Frank Little was a renowned figure within the IWW, greatly admired for his fearless dedication to the union. By 1917, he had been organizing in the field for more than a decade, having suffered numerous beatings and having served several stints in jail. Little was not widely known outside of the union. Short and wiry, he neither possessed a commanding presence nor projected as a charismatic speaker. Still, he commanded the respect of miners throughout the West for his integrity and courage, as well as his abilities as an organizer.

Little was born in 1877 in a small town in Illinois. His mother was one-quarter Indian, probably Cherokee. The family moved to the newly opened Oklahoma Territory in 1889. By a decade later, Little had become a copper miner in Arizona, where he soon became active in the Western Federation of Miners, traveling around the state as a union organizer. Initially, the WFM affiliated with the IWW, but in 1907 it withdrew its affiliation. When Little sided with the Wobblies, he was fired as a WFM organizer. He then became an IWW organizer, and was arrested during the Spokane free speech fight in 1909 and during a similar battle in Fresno in 1910. Having established his reputation within the union, Little was elected to the General Executive Board in 1911, retaining this post until his death.

In 1916, Little was kidnapped by vigilantes while organizing iron miners on the Mesabi Range in northern Minnesota, badly beaten and nearly lynched before being released. Undaunted, he came to Arizona to lead the organizing drive of Southwestern copper miners. His stay in Arizona would lead to his most successful organizing effort, as the IWW's Metal Mine Workers' Industrial Union #800 quickly established large, active branches in the key mining districts.

Little was not only fearless in the face of violence, he had the courage to hold to his principles in the face of government repression. When the U.S. declared war on Germany in April 1917, he demanded that the IWW continue to actively oppose the war. To the end, Little remained adamant, insisting that the union had the obligation to organize against the war effort, despite the likelihood that this would make the IWW a prime target of the federal government.

Little spent the last weeks of his life in Butte, Montana. His time in Butte was marked by limited success. Butte's strike leaders were veteran organizers and they were convinced that the situation in that district was different from that in other mining districts. Although they respected Little, they were also insistent that key decisions would be made by Butte's activists and not by an outside organizer. Thus, Little had a minimal impact on the direction of the Butte strike. Still, he spoke out in forceful opposition to the war, while most of Butte's union leaders avoided the issue.

On the night of August 1, 1917, a death squad in the employ of the mining companies abducted Little, dragged him by a rope from a moving car and then lynched him. No one was ever prosecuted for this cold-blooded, brutal assassination.

To this day, Frank Little remains the symbol of the IWW in its heyday.

Battling Injuries

Over the course of his fifteen years of organizing, Little had been severely beaten several times by local police and corporate gunmen. By the time he arrived in Arizona in January 1917, Little was approaching forty and his health was fragile. Soon afterward, he traveled to El Paso, Texas to organize workers at a smelter. He was again assaulted by police before being ordered to leave town. This time the beating caused a ruptured hernia.

For the next months, until his death, Little suffered acute pain as he traveled to the various mining camps in Arizona. At times, his morale plummeted. In addition to the intense pain, he felt that he was being ignored and that the Arizona organizing drive was not being given the support it should have received from Bill Haywood and the Chicago headquarters. Nevertheless, the transcript documents indicate that Haywood and the General Executive Board appreciated Little's organizing efforts and were ready to pay for the surgical operation he needed.

The following correspondence reveal a very human side of Frank Little, as well as the respect he had earned from union activists for his dedication and his willingness to sacrifice his health for the sake of the union.

DOCUMENT ONE

Letter

Frank Little to Grover Perry

Jerome, Ariz. Apr. 11, 1917

Grover H. Perry
Phoenix, Ariz.

Fellow Worker:

Enclosed find name of three members who have transferred into #800. W. McIntyre, card #94792 from #493. Swansia. Dues paid for June 1917. Terry O'Brien from #621 to #800. Card #263176. Int. Jan 8, 1911. Dues paid for May 1917. You have the book of 693 and 621 in the office. Walter M. Weise, card #204579, from #602 to #800. Int. Jan 10, 1917. Send his transfer notice to Los Angeles.[1]

I arrived here yesterday evening. If we can get a hall will hold meeting, but it is doubtful. Pedro Coria is needed here bad, him or some Mexican. Joe Oates says he is going to get a job and get a piece of money to live on. He cannot live on the wages he gets and–well I know that. I wish Haywood and some of the others who opposed giving the org. an increase had to live in the mining camps on the wages we get. I am writing Haywood today to send one of the board members or some one else to take my place, as I am no longer able to do the work. My health is completely gone; cannot be on my feet only an hour or two at a time, when I must lay down, and the organization cannot afford to pay wages to a sick man.

If I can get a new truss, might hold me for a while; think I will get out in the hills and prospect, if I can get some one to grub stake me.[2] The only show I see to get money to fix myself up and Joe Oates showed me the bulletin, but you failed to put Donnelly[3] in.

Yours for Ind Freedom,
F.H. Little

IWW Trial Transcript, pp. 7922-24

DOCUMENT TWO

Letter

Grover Perry to Frank Little

April 13, 1917

Mr. F.H. Little
Box K
Jerome, Arizona

Fellow Worker:

I have yours of the 11th, and contents have been carefully noted.

I wrote Oates, and told him I would allow his $7.00 a week expenses, in addition to the $18 per [week].[4] I know that I have no authority to take such a step, but Oates has turned in about two dollars to every dollar that he has taken out of the office, and we need men like him in the field. I am going to presume on my power a little, and boost wages when necessary to keep men like him going. If the rank and file wish to 'can' me for so doing, it will be nothing new in my experience as I have known the pleasure of having the 'can' tied to me many times.

Note that you wrote Haywood telling him that you want to get out. I received an answer from Haywood in [response to] the letter I sent him. He said that he was going to put the matter up to the Executive Board, and if the Executive Board didn't come across, we would have to raise it some other way. He said he would put in a ten spot toward the operation himself. If you can not stand the work in town, it is a 'lead pipe cinch' that you can not stand the racket in the desert. If you are feeling very bad, come to Phoenix. We will get rooms with an extra bed, and I think my wife and I can stand the 'star boarder' for a few months, at least.

Will send you a photograph of some W.F.M. cards in a day or so.

With Best Wishes, I am,
Yours for Industrial Freedom
Sec'y Treas. 800

IWW Trial Transcript, pp. 7919-20

DOCUMENT THREE

Motion

Francis Miller

GENERAL EXECUTIVE BOARD

Motion:

That inasmuch as Frank Little was injured while working for the Organization, and his condition renders an operation necessary; that the expenses attending to said opposition be defrayed from the General Fund.

Francis Miller, G.E.B.

I, Francis Miller, member of the General Executive Board record my vote on the above referendum as follows: Yes

IWW Trial Transcript, p.10901

DOCUMENT FOUR

Letter

Frank Little to Grover Perry

May 17, 1917

Grover H. Perry
Phoenix, Ariz.

Fellow Worker:

Yours of 15th at hand. Note what you say regarding Globe and Miami. That place, as I told you, has gone to hell since [the] war craze started. I can not understand Bob Williams, and then [although] Bob was selected by me before you put Cuhr on. As soon as I left, he, as you know, laid down; as to Cuhr, he is not able to tramp over the hills. I knew that at the time I had you put Williams on the job, but he is acquainted with the miners; as to getting [a] job delegate there at this time, it is out of the question. I found it so before I left, for to be known as an I.W.W. is to get fired; that was my reason for wanting Joe Oates to stay there. Now is the hard period; if we can pull through for a couple or three months, things will change. To do anything here, we must have a delegate on the payroll. I do not have anyone here who will act as delegate. The G.O[5] must aid; for my part am sorry I ever came, that we ever started to organize the miners. I supposed we would have the assistance of the G.O. as I knew we would have all kinds of opposition. I have written Bill [Haywood] several letters but he ignores me; will not tell me anything; I am damn tired of it, have written him several times to send some one in my place. Some one whom he can trust and work with; there must be some one here; I can not stay here, as I must go to new country if we [are to] accomplish anything. Baskett would be a good man; am writing Haywood, asking the G.O. to come through with some money to pay at least one half of his wages and expenses.

As far as I am concerned, I am not able to do the work, so why pay a sick man; get some one who can stand the gaff, and who can bring in the goods. I can not hike over the hills; it knocks me out to ride in an auto. I have got to quit; I want to take in the northern part of the state, and I am not able to go the route. If I was able to get out and defy the Powers that be, I could start something, but a jolt behind the bars now would finish me. You say for me not to think of quitting, what in hell else can I do? I was told that the Attorney General has under consideration my arrest for treason; maybe the government would operate on me if arrested.

There is a lad in Prescott who is on the sick list, had his eye blowed out; has suit against the Co. He is behind [in his dues]. Paid up until the first of the year. I transferred him from 73 the other trip.

He says several miners have come to him wanting to join, or pay dues. It would be a good idea to send him supplies. I told him to use the Commission to fix up his card. His name is J.P. O'Malley. Brinkmeyer Hotel, Prescott Ariz; write to him.

Are the *El Rebelde*, *Sol* and *Worker* supposed to come here?[6] If so, they are not coming. Send me the latest *Sol* and *Worker*, [and] some application blanks. Send me the name of [the] delegate in the north part of the state.

Yours for Ind Freedom
F.H. Little

P.S.: Enc. M.O. 26.45 and $2.00 check from 400 Dist-Edwards. Say what that check was, I don't know what it was sent to me for. Will keep tab on the application signed by Brown. You can send him check later for the Comishiner.

IWW Trial Transcript, pp. 7952-54

DOCUMENT FIVE

Letter

Frank Little to Grover Perry

Jerome, Ariz. 6/4/17

Grover H. Perry
Phoenix, Ariz.

Fellow Worker:

Your letter with check received, but there were no blank credentials. I need them. We had a good meeting. I went strong and I was [good]; I may [have been] too strong for my own good, as we had government agents present.

Baskett will be over Tuesday; I will stay with him for a few days, [and] then will be down to Phoenix.

Feel sore. We will have a large influx of members [on] pay day; it is mail time; will close; write you again in a few days.

Yours for Ind. Freedom,
F.H. Little

IWW Trial Transcript, p. 7970

Assisting the Strike of Copper Miners

On June 20, 1917, Little was traveling by car from Bisbee to the Globe-Miami district. When the car was driven over a cliff, Little was again injured, suffering a broken bone in his right ankle. After a brief stay in the hospital, he spent several days in a secluded cabin recovering from the accident. Little then traveled to Chicago, on crutches, for a meeting of the General Executive Board, never to return to Arizona.

Still, the following letter indicates that Little continued to closely follow events in Arizona while in Chicago, providing advice to Grover Perry on strategy and tactics to be followed during the strike.

DOCUMENT SIX

Letter

Frank Little to Grover Perry

Chicago, Ill.
June 29, 1917

Grover H. Perry
Box 10
Phoenix, Ariz.

Fellow Worker:

Well, old top, from the news I have received since I arrived in Chi, you must be having some busy times. Sorry I am not with you; was rather sorry to hear the miners pulled the stunt so quick.[7] Think it would have been better if they had waited until the Organization Committee of 800 got things in working order, and gotten their plans laid to call a general strike. Of course, if the boys wanted to go, it would never do to try to hold them back. I wish you would keep me posted as to the conditions there.

The board is all here. Just getting through with the books; so far I have been taking it easy, not doing much of anything; hope we will soon get down to the important work.

Had Bill wire to Thompson to drop all speaking dates, and rush to Ariz. Hope Lena is getting well. Let me hear from you as soon and [as] often as you have time. If it is necessary, as soon as the meeting is over, I will postpone the operation and jump back to the desert.

Yours for Ind. Freedom,
F. H. Little

IWW Trial Transcript, pp. 7968-9

Butte

As soon as the meeting of the General Executive Board ended, Little proceeded to Butte, Montana, stopping in Salt Lake City to briefly meet with Grover Perry. Butte was the largest, and most productive, copper mining district in the world. On June 8, 1917, a fire had swept through one of the mines, killing 167. Thousands of infuriated miners responded by walking off the job as production stopped throughout the district. Miners came together to form a new, independent union, demanding its recognition and the end of the rustling card system whereby the Anaconda Copper Mining Company, the dominant company in Butte, screened out union militants.

Butte had a long history of militant unionism and radical politics. The new union was controlled by radicals, but only some of them were sympathizers of the IWW. Another informal group was aligned with the left-wing of the Socialist Party and had no desire to see the new union affiliate with the IWW. Haywood had previously dispatched a series of organizers to Butte in the weeks since the strike had started, hoping that they would convince the independent union, the Butte Metal Mine Workers' Union, to affiliate with the IWW. All of these efforts had been rebuffed.

Little was therefore in an awkward situation, He was treated with respect, and given the unique honor of addressing a mass rally of miners. Nevertheless, there was no chance that the new union would agree to affiliate with the IWW. Furthermore, as veteran activists the leaders of the independent union were unwilling to accept Little's advice on strategy and tactics.

The following letter indicates that Little soon realized the limitations of his influence. Developing a close working relationship with Butte's community of activist miners would require a long-term commitment and would not be the outcome of a brief visit.

DOCUMENT SEVEN

Letter

Frank Little to Grover Perry

Butte, Montana, July 24, 1917

Grover H. Perry
Room 506 Boyd Park Building
Salt Lake City, Utah

Fellow Worker:

We have just opened an office; have got several delegates out working. I will take charge of the office for a time, and working with the Finnish members. Things are looking a lot better for the I.W.W. The boys tell me that a short time ago one could not mention the three letters without getting thrown out of meetings, but now we have good crowds at our meetings. We hold three propaganda meetings a week.

In our work with the members of the new union, we will be compelled to ignore the [IWW] Constitution regarding the taking up of the Metal Mine Workers cards. I am accepting their cards in lieu of initiation fees, and allowing them to retain their cards. Will have the application signed by two or more delegates, vouching for the fact that they have the card of the M.M.U. That is the [only] way they [the miners] accept the I.W.W. Card. While I am sure we will take up all their cards later on, for they will all come in to the M.M.W.U. 800, we must make no false moves. This is a damn hard place to handle, but I am making good headway, and will have a good bunch of English speaking delegates.

How are things moving? What is the news from Ariz., haven't heard anything from them since I left the Lake. Is the relief coming in yet? As soon as you have any relief money, you can send some up here, but send it to the Finns; they will handle the I.W.W. relief from this end.

Did Fred Moore get to Ariz. yet. I am afraid some of the boys there are up against it pretty hard. Have you anyone there who can handle the affairs? I am still unable to get around much, I have a room next door to the hall, so I can handle this alright. There are some of the parasites who are doing all they can to cause my arrest, but so far they have failed. Keep me posted on what is doing? Will write you every few days, and let me know ho things are moving here.

> Yours for Ind. Freedom,
> F.H. Little
> G.E.B. Member

IWW Trial Transcript, pp. 7979-80

While in Butte, Little continued to badger Haywood to agree that the IWW should commit its resources to fostering an active resistance to the war and the draft. Little was convinced that the union had an obligation to carry through its principled opposition to militarism and conscription. The following letters reveal the deepening divide between Little and Haywood on issues related to the war.

DOCUMENT EIGHT

Letter[8]
Frank Little to William Haywood

Butte, Mont., July 24, 1917

William D. Haywood
Chicago, Ill.

Fellow Worker:

When will the statement of the Board on the war be out. It should be sent to members as soon as possible. Let me hear from you soon. Give me the news of the movement.

> F.H. Little
> G.E.B. Member

DOCUMENT NINE

Letter[9]

William Haywood to Frank Little

July 27, 1917

F.H. Little
Butte, Mont.

Fellow Worker:

In regard to the statement of the board on war, will say, after the statement in this week's *Solidarity* by the editor, it would be superfluous to publish the statement of the Board, as it is practically the same and covers the same essential points as '*Solidarity*'s' statement.

General Sec.-Treas.

DOCUMENT TEN

Letter[10]

Frank Little to William Haywood

Butte, Montana, July 30, 1917

William D. Haywood
Chicago, Ill.

Fellow Worker:

Yours of the 27 received this morning. Haven't received Charter for Branc[h] yet. Note what you say regarding the Report of the Board on the war. But do not agree with you. The statement of *Sol* was not from the Board, and I insist that there should be a statement from the Board as to their stand on this and all other wars; it is my opinion that it should go [out] at once.

F.H. Little
G.E.B. Member

The following letter may be the last Little wrote. During his last hours, he was still suffering a great deal of pain from a ruptured hernia, but he had stopped even considering the possibility of resigning. On the contrary, Little was preparing to remain in Montana for some time, splitting his time between Butte and the timber camps of northwestern Montana, where the IWW's Lumber Workers' Industrial Union #500 was still engaged in a lengthy strike.

DOCUMENT ELEVEN

Letter

Frank Little to Grover Perry

Butte Montana, July 30, 1917

Grover H. Perry
Salt Lake City, Utah

Fellow Worker:
Yours of the 28 with check for 35.00 received this morning. Enclosed find statement of wages and expenses for week ending July 28, 1917.

Sec'ty of Branch is sending in report this morning, not a great deal of money, as we have some printing bills to pay, and you must remember the miners here now has no money. The members of the I.W.W. have had no relief from the outside up to this time. Neither have any of them made any kick as they realize the I.W.W. has an awful job on their hands, but if the strike was to last for any length of time, they will have to have some aid. The Finns has sent an appeal to the Finnish paper to be sent to you.

The strike looks better this morning than any time since I arrived. The spirit of the miners is good. I am of the opinion that some of my Double Jack[11] blows I have given them, from the I.W.W. view point, has had its effect. Some of the so-called leaders seem to be afraid of me. That comes from the continual hammering that the capitalist press gives me.

Will take a trip to the other parts of the country in a few days. Will go to Missoula, where the timber for the mining companies comes from. The lumber workers want me for some dates, but at this time I feel that most of my time should at the present be with the miners. I am on my last page, walking on these sticks isn't doing my rupture any good. The strain on me is sometimes more than I can stand.

What is the news from Ariz? I haven't heard a word, have written and wired but get no reply. Send me any news you have, would like to take a trip to that country, but I know it would be a waste of time and money, for in the condition I am in I could never get to any of the mining camps, so I will do the best I can.

Bastain, you know him, is here working out of Spokane. He is going out on a job. If he doesn't get his check today, [I] will loan the money to him from the Branch, send you my receipt and you can hold it for me.

Hope Lena is getting well.[12] Hello to my Pal.

Yours for Ind Freedom,
F.H. Little,
G.E.B. Member

IWW Trial Transcript, pp. 7983-84

Assassination

Little must have known that he was in immediate danger while in Butte. Still, he was determined to stay, and to see out the miners' strike. In the early hours of August 1, Little was kidnapped from his boarding house by six masked men, with a seventh waiting in a car. He was beaten unconscious, and then dragged by a rope from a moving car for more than a mile. Frank Little was then lynched, hanged from a railroad trestle on the outskirts of Butte. The assassins, gunmen hired by the mining companies, were never prosecuted.

COPPER TRUST TO THE PRESS: "IT'S ALL RIGHT, PAL; JUST TELL THEM HE WAS A TRAITOR."

"Just Tell Them He Was a Traitor"
Ralph Chaplin, *Solidarity*, August 11, 1917

The following song was written by the wife of Frank Little's brother Fred shortly after Little was murdered. Emma Little was an IWW activist in California. Frank Little often stayed with Emma and Fred, resting from the stresses of organizing for the IWW.

DOCUMENT TWELVE

Song

Tune: "Count Your Blessings"

Emma B. Little, *Solidarity*, August 18, 1917

Bring Out the White Wash

Don't read the Declaration, boys, it's un-American[13]
That's what the cops will tell you in little old Spokane
Instead of the Constitution, Post Mortems now you'll get[14]
The capitalists are killing off the working men, you bet
    Bring out the white wash
    Bring out the white wash
    Spread it on as thick as you can
    Bring out the white wash
    Bring out the white wash
            We've murdered another working man

Down in Bisbee town you ought to see the fun
When we rounded up the working men and made the Bisbee run
And while we were about it, we took all their cash
We knew they would[n't] need it, in the desert there's no hash

Chorus

Frank Little was an agitator, he made the people think
We thought we'd better get him or else he'd raise a stink
And so we planned the murder well, the cops were nowhere near
They, everyone, had gone to get another glass of beer

Chorus

We've got another bunch picked out, and we will get them too
We've planned the murders carefully, and just how we will do
There'll be no interference, for the cops will all be wise
We're killing off the working men because they organize

Within hours after the murder, the Butte Metal Mine Workers' Union was quite certain of the names of those who had participated in the lynching, and their ties to the mining companies. They issued the following statement, and yet the union never publicly named the killers or provided evidence of the complicity of the mining companies. There was no investigation, and no prosecutions, so the assassins remained free. The mining companies, and the Rockefeller interests behind them, were too powerful. They could literally get away with murder.

DOCUMENT THIRTEEN

Article

August 11, 1917

Solidarity

Butte, Mont. Aug. 2, 1917

Sunday morning, August 1, at three o'clock, a working man was dragged from his bed, thrown into an automobile, taken to the outskirts of the city and hanged.

Without a word of warning, giving him less chance than would be given a dog, a man-a cripple-was hurled into eternity by a gang of the most cowardly degenerates that ever disgraced this earth-contemptible, despicable brutes who hid their faces behind masks that no one might see them.

And before Little's body was cold, there were extras on the streets denouncing him, and hurling columns of filthy lies and abuse at the corpse of the man murdered by gunmen and thugs of even lower type than the editors of these lying sheets.

And we hear constantly preached, by the same murderous assassins, the fairy tale of "Law and Order."

What a mockery! What a fiendish conception of freedom!

No other country in this so-called civilized world has ever been disgraced by such open and flagrant violations of all law.

Nowhere else would such outrages be tolerated by the authorities.

We are conducting an investigation of this murder and already have sufficient evidence to indicate the names of five men who took part, everyone of whom is a company stool pigeon. Two of these men are in business, two are gunmen, and one is connected with LAW ENFORCEMENT in this city.

We have already found that certain people saw the automobile loaded with men, recognized some of them, are able to identify the others, and, above all, are anxious to do so.

Threats have already been made that if we succeed in proving who committed the crime, we will never live to tell it. We want to inform them that three copies of every bit of information we have are deposited in three different places to be used in case they succeed in getting any of us.

WE KNOW ALREADY THAT ALIBIS WERE PREPARED IN ADVANCE FOR EVERY ONE OF THE MURDERERS. YET WE HAVE EVIDENCE THAT WILL BREAK EVERY ALIBI COMPLETELY.

AND WHEN WE FINISH, SOME VERY PROMINENT MURDERERS WILL BE HEADED FOR THE GALLOWS OR DEER LODGE.

AND EVEN THE POWERFUL INFLUENCES BEHIND THEM WILL NOT AVAIL TO SAVE THEM.

―――

We know that this murder is designed to strike terror in the hearts, not only of the men whose initials are printed on the infamous placard, but to that of every independent man in this community who has ever shown any spirit of independence.[15]

It has failed to frighten anyone, and has resulted in aligning the support and the sympathy of everyone with the Metal Mine Workers' Union.

Every effort will be made by the daily press to clear the skirts of the Company, BUT EVERY MAN, WOMAN AND CHILD IN THIS COUNTY KNOWS THAT COMPANY AGENTS PERPETRATED THIS FOULEST OF ALL CRIMES.

We want the police to know that this is the culmination of a series of brutal assaults committed by Company gunmen upon members of our union, and that in many instances women and children have been beaten and threatened.

Every morning and evening for the past seven weeks, but particularly for about two weeks, crowds of gunmen have gathered on East Granite and East Broadway, where, without excuse or reason, they have beaten, abused and insulted men, women and children.

The papers each night and morning have been filled with stories charging all manner of offenses against every one living in the district mentioned.

Wm. Oates, Herman Gillis (son of the former postmaster, Malcolm Gillis), Pete Boudin, a rat named Middleton, and about two dozen others, working under a chief gunman named Ryan, have been particularly active.

Complaint after complaint has been made to the authorities, and no attention paid, until finally the county attorney was compelled to file a charge against Oates, who was seen by twenty witnesses to knock a man down, and tear the watch out of his pocket, breaking the chain and stealing the watch.

Two and three gunmen have made it a practice to attack single men and beat them into insensibility.

This has been done systematically in the hope of provoking us into active resistance, so that they might shoot us down and break the strike by instituting a reign of terror.

We have known from the start what they wanted, and have refused to fall for it; consequently, in desperation, the companies were obliged to stage this murder.

As a result of the policy of the Union, our members all realized exactly what the companies are trying to do, and when the news was spread that Little was dead, every man's coolness was immediately manifest.

Even when the extra paper appeared, containing only vilification of the dead man, no one was carried away by rage or resentment.

Instead, a cool, calm relentless determination to trace the crime to its source, and punish not only the actual perpetrators, but those who directed them as well.

The Post, true to its jackal instincts, abuses the dead man, endeavoring to create the impression that he was in imminent danger of arrest by United States authorities for making treasonable remarks.

The actual facts are: The local federal officials, induced by complaints made by company agents, thoroughly investigated the alleged treasonable statements of Frank Little and found absolutely nothing to warrant a prosecution.

Not one violation of the law. Yet a gang of degenerates, cowardly brutes, seized him, and, as the autopsy shows, after putting him into the automobile, tied a rope around his neck, threw him out of the car, dragged him to the place where he was found, beat him, and when they were tired of torturing the poor cripple-HANGED HIM.

AND TODAY-THOSE DOGS, THOSE FIENDS IN HUMAN FORM, THOSE COWARDLY, DEGENERATE BRUTES, ARE WALKING THE STREETS OF BUTTE-HAVING REPORTED TO THE MEN WHO ARE BEHIND THEM THAT THEY SUCCEEDED IN MURDERING A MAN WITH A BROKEN LEG.

―――

Jeannette Rankin[16] telegraphed, reporting her horror of this latest crime, and assuring us that she is going to enlist federal aid.

―――

This crime, more than any other, should teach the people of Butte that it is time to demand that Company rule in Butte should be broken. Every workingman must feel that it is time to back us to the last ditch.

SO LONG AS ANY MAN CAN BE MURDERED AS LITTLE HAS BEEN, NO MAN IS SAFE.

No thought was given to his mother and loved ones, and no more would be given you and yours than was given Little.

We are up against a murderous, bloodthirsty gang of dogs, who would strangle their own mothers or families if the Company told them to.

THE WAY TO PREVENT SUCH OUTRAGES IS
BY THOROUGH ORGANIZATION.

DO YOU BELIEVE THAT SUCH CRIMES SHOULD
BE PERPETRATED?

DO YOU KNOW THAT YOU OR SOMEONE DEAR
TO YOU MAY BE THE NEXT?

GET BUSY! SUPPORT US IN OUR FIGHT!

NO MAN IS SAFE!

SECTION THREE : WORLD WAR I

Opposing the War

Opposition to militarism and imperialism had always been a fundamental tenet of the IWW, starting with its formation in 1905. Indeed, deepening the solidarity of the working class across national boundaries was a primary goal of the union. Wobbly newspapers printed articles and editorials denouncing U.S. imperial adventures, while the union's song book featured anti-militarist lyrics. Even after the start of World War I, the union continued to advance an anti-militarist perspective. The 1916 delegate convention reaffirmed this position and IWW leaders remained vociferous in their criticisms of the war.

In April 1917, when the United States entered the war as a combatant, the IWW was confronted with a drastically altered landscape. A decision to uphold its previous position would, in all likelihood, trigger a direct confrontation with the federal government. IWW leaders quickly understood the choice that confronted them following the official declaration of war on Germany.

Haywood immediately shifted his position, urging caution, while issuing repeated warnings that the union had no option but to drop its militant opposition to the war if it were to survive the wartime crisis. His position was supported by virtually all of the leaders of the industrial unions affiliated with the IWW. With the economy in high gear producing weapons and equipment for a huge army, labor markets were tight, thus giving workers greater leverage. Furthermore, workers in the Western states were ready to listen to the union's message of radical politics and militant industrial unionism. Wobbly officials eagerly believed that the war had provided the union with a tremendous opportunity, one that would be placed in jeopardy by any organized effort to oppose the war effort.

Rank and file Wobblies saw the situation in a very different light. They were incensed by President Woodrow Wilson's decision to push the country into a global war. Many of them would be drafted to fight in a bloodbath that they viewed as an inter-imperialist squabble. Union militants repeatedly wrote to the headquarters of IWW affiliated unions urging officials to be more vocal in their opposition to the war. In general, Wobbly activists were told that the union would, and could, do nothing. IWW leaders generally contended that as long as the union was not in a position to call an effective general strike, it could not stop the war and thus the immediate priority had to be organizing in the workplace.

This rationale ducked the real questions. After all, prior to 1917 the IWW had repeatedly condemned imperialism and militarism, even though it did not have the organized strength to insist upon a different foreign policy. The truth was that the IWW was abandoning its previous position for reasons of expediency, a reality understood by those on both sides of the issue.

The issue simmered throughout the spring and summer of 1917. This can be seen most acutely in a series of letters exchanged between Bill Haywood and Frank Little. The interchange was acrimonious, as Little made it very clear that Haywood was betraying the core principles of the union.

Little was convinced that the IWW had the moral obligation to try to stop the war, although he also realized that this principled position would lead the union to become a focus of government repression. In July 1917, Little presented a militant anti-war resolution to the General Executive Board, but Haywood was able to block its passage. Instead, Haywood and the GEB decided that the union should affiliate with the People's Council of America, a loose coalition of liberals and moderate socialists, which organized around a call for a negotiated peace.

In its attempt to avoid controversy, the IWW wound up floundering, falling short on every count. Its efforts to oppose the war were tentative and half-hearted. Nevertheless, careful as the union's leaders were, the government was still infuriated by the effective strikes conducted by the IWW in key industries. In spite of Haywood's cautious policies, the IWW became the target of a ruthless, coordinated campaign of repression by the federal government.

Opposition to Militarism Reaffirmed

The IWW had no doubt where it stood when World War I first began in August 1914. IWW activists were convinced that the union could not restrict its focus to workplace issues, and that it had to maintain its stance of militant opposition to militarism. Through a variety of methods, the union distributed propaganda ridiculing both sides of the conflict, while portraying the war as an imperialist conflict that could only benefit the bankers and the munition makers.

"Not Yet, It Still Pays"
Ernest Riebe. *Solidarity*, October 3, 1914

In December 1916, when delegates assembled in Chicago for the the convention, everyone was aware that opposition to the war might soon lead the union into a direct confrontation with the federal government. Bill Haywood joined with Frank Little and two others in proposing a resolution that reaffirmed the IWW's total opposition to war and pledged that the union would continue to organize militant protests even after war was declared.[1] The resolution was passed overwhelmingly, with little opposition.

In February 1917, the executive council of the American Federation of Labor approved a resolution pledging enthusiastic and uncritical support of the war effort. Haywood then ordered the printing of 20,000 copies of a leaflet titled "Deadly Parallel," setting the two resolutions in opposite columns, directly contrasting them. This leaflet was also printed in the front page of the March 24, 1917 issue of *Solidarity*. Once it became certain that the United States would enter the war, Haywood retreated. As General Secretary-Treasurer, he insisted that the thousands of copies of the leaflet be withdrawn from circulation, and he made sure that there was no further mention of the 1916 convention resolution, which he had sponsored, in any IWW newspaper.

DOCUMENT ONE

Resolution of the 10th General Convention of the IWW[2]
December 1916

A DECLARATION

We, the Industrial Workers of the World, in convention assembled, hereby reaffirm our adherence to the principle of Industrial Unionism, and rededicate ourselves to the unflinching, unfaltering prosecution of the struggle for the abolition of wage slavery and the realization of our ideal in Industrial Democracy. With the European war for conquest and exploitation raging and destroying the lives, class consciousness and unity of the workers, and the ever-growing agitation for military preparedness clouding the main issues and delaying the realization of our ultimate aim with patriotic, and, therefore, capitalistic aspirations, we openly declare ourselves the determined opponents of all nationalistic sectionalism, or patriotism, and the militarism preached and supported by our one enemy, the capitalist class. We condemn all wars, and for the prevention of such, we proclaim the anti-militarist propaganda in time of peace, thus promoting Class Solidarity among the workers of the entire world, and, in time of war, the General Strike in all industries. We extend assurances of both moral and material support to all the workers who suffer at the hands of the capitalist class for their adhesion to these principles, and call on all workers to unite themselves with us, that the reign of the exploiters may cease and this earth be made fair through the establishment of the Industrial Democracy.

General Headquarters Shifts its Position

The Congressional vote to declare war on Germany in April 1917 placed the IWW in a difficult dilemma. The resolution approved by the convention only a few months earlier committed the union to a policy of militant resistance to the war effort. The implementation of this pledge would guarantee that the union would be targeted for harsh repressive measures by the federal government.

Haywood immediately dropped his support for a policy of resistance, and instead urged the union to proceed with caution, having determined that the priority had to be the survival of the union. The following editorial written by Ralph Chaplin as editor of *Solidarity*, at the behest of Haywood, lays out the new position. Organizing against the war, and against the draft, was a mere "distraction" from the primary task of organizing at the workplace.

DOCUMENT TWO

Editorial

Solidarity, April 7, 1917[3]

RENEWED I.W.W. ACTIVITY

War is looming up more menacingly each day. The greatest campaign this country has ever seen is being pushed in an organized manner to lash the newspaper-made spirit of militarism to a frenzy. Also, the authorities of several western states are attempting to legally suppress the I.W.W. under the mask of their "anti-criminal syndicalist" laws.

And still the I.W.W. refuses to be distracted from the main issue of the big fight, the organization of the workers on the job to obtain job control and all that goes with it.

Neither is the defense of our loyal fellow workers in jail being neglected, and it must not be overlooked, even momentarily. These members of the One Big Union are relying upon us to do for them what they would do for us were the conditions reversed.

Let us start with renewed vigor and increased enthusiasm to make this the banner year for the organization, and let us work as we have never worked before to free our fellow workers from the clutches of the enemy.

As much as we abhor the wars of the master class, we cannot afford to have the great work of ORGANIZATION sidetracked into an anti-militarism groove. As much as we dislike to see the law-making puppets of the bosses seek to enmesh our efforts to organize the slaves in a network of "legal" opposition, we must not forget that we can and will go ahead with our work just as though nothing had happened. And the defense of the brave boys in jail is not to be lost in the shuffle.

Don't forget that the Sab Cat has ninety-nine lives and that the I.W.W. is unkillable.

Raymond Fanning was a young activist new to radical politics. Fanning wrote to the IWW headquarters seeking advice on how to respond to the decision to enter the war. Harrison George worked on *Solidarity*, while assisting Haywood in the Chicago office. His response to Fanning presents the union leadership's rationale for not helping to organize against the war.

DOCUMENT THREE

Letter

Harrison George to Raymond Fanning

Chicago, Ill., April 17, 1917

Ray S. Fanning
Box 91
Chattanooga, Tenn.

Fellow Worker:

You will find a receipt enclosed for the money sent for subs which will be entered on our list at once.

We appreciate your compliment on our stand upon the war question. We are not paying much attention to the little war the masters have decided for the scissors to fight. The BIG THING is the CLASS WAR. Should they insist that we suspend the Class War then is when the fun will begin, and the Old Cat will likely have kittens.

We have no sub cards for the new address, but will send you a sub book and you may use it for combination offers, or club offers the same as if you use cards. We would like to have news from that part of the world, [so] send something small and juicy now and then, and we will try to run it. You know—job news, etc.

Yours for Ours,
SOLIDARITY
Harrison George

IWW Trial Transcript, p. 12090

The IWW at Odds

Virtually all IWW militants opposed the war and were eager for union to become actively involved in organizing against it. On the other hand, most of the leaders of the industrial unions affiliated with the IWW wanted the union to avoid taking any public stance on the war, concentrating instead on organizing at the workplace.

Throughout the spring and summer of 1917, rank and file Wobblies repeatedly wrote to union officials urging them to act. There pleas for action were summarily rejected. The following letter provides another response to Raymond Fanning's request for advice on how to respond to the war. Walter Nef was one of the most influential IWW leaders. As the first secretary of the Agricultural Workers' Organization, he had devised the delegate system by which union activists were charged with collecting dues and initiation fees in isolated farms and timber camps and then forwarding this money to union headquarters. Nef had been transferred to Philadelphia where he acted as secretary of the Maritime Workers' Industrial Union. Although he was one of the more cautious IWW officials, Nef's response to Fanning nevertheless typifies the official response to rank and file calls for the union to speak out against the war.

DOCUMENT FOUR

Letter

Walter Nef to Raymond Fanning

Philadelphia, PA.
April 3rd, 1917

Raymond S. Fanning
Box 91
Chattanooga, Tenn.

Fellow Worker:

Received your letter of the 31st and the M.O. of 90c, and you will find a receipt from same enclosed. Regards the dues books and stamps, you pay for that as you use it. That's the way we do [it], unless a delegate has too much money, and wants to keep some on deposit here.

Regards to the matter of this country going to war with Germany, will state [that] the I.W.W. cannot stop it at this time, as the workers are not organized yet in this country nor in the other countries. It is true that we are against war, and against all wars, [but] the workers must first be organized to stop any war before they are effective in doing so. Cannot give any advice what to do, as circumstances and conditions continually change.

With best wishes, I am yours for the One Big Union,
W.T. Nef
Secy-Treas M.T.W. 100

IWW Trial Transcript, pp. 12052-3

The debate was particularly intense within the Lumber Workers' Industrial Union #500 where lumberjacks were on strike throughout the Pacific Northwest. Herbert Mahler was one of the leaders of the union. The following letter was written only days after the U.S. declared war on Germany. Mahler urges the union to proceed cautiously in distributing anti-war literature, while promising that at some undefined future date it will become more forthright in its opposition.

DOCUMENT FIVE

Letter

Herbert Mahler to Harry Lloyd

Seattle, Wash., April 10, 1917

Harry Lloyd
27 N. First St.
Portland, Oregon
Fellow Worker:

Your letter of April 8th enclosing $15.00 donation to the Everett defense received. Enclosed find receipt for same.

It is good to know that most of the boys are out on the job.

As you say, the war question will undoubtedly hold back the labor movement to an extent. I see by this morning's paper that they are already howling for conscription. When the conscription issue comes up, I expect that the I.W.W. will fight hard. Until we have that situation to meet with however, I think it would be wise to go a little easy on the anti-militarism propaganda. Our aims are to prevent militarism and war through organization, and while we are not openly declaring ourselves against the war, I think that it will be doing more to prevent future occasions like this by steadily going on with our efforts toward organization.

The masters are undoubtedly looking for an opportunity to close down some of our halls, and if we do give them an excuse we should be sure to give them a damn good one. The M. & M.[4] here are circulating a circular with the 'Onward Christian Soldier" song on it and, at the bottom, calling on all patriotic citizens to see that this terrible I.W.W. is wiped out. They are not having much success however. Their great patriotic parade of Saturday night was a fizzle. I doubt if they have recruited three hundred men to date.

The general feeling of the working class here is against the war. While they are not declaring themselves openly, they are showing it by refusing to enlist, and refusing to give any assistance to demonstrations calculated to encourage enlistments.

With best wishes to all the boys, I remain
Yours for Industrial Freedom,
Herbert Mahler

IWW Trial Transcript, pp. 15415-15416

The following correspondence comes again from the Lumber Workers' Union. Joseph Ratti was a delegate in one of the small timber communities in located in the northwestern corner of Montana. He had, undoubtedly, been vocal in his opposition to the war. The IWW had, therefore, become a target for zealous patriots who insisted that the the U.S. flag be displayed at the union hall. Ratti wanted to resist this coerced support for a war he detested, but Don Sheridan, as interim secretary of the LWIU, advised Ratti to comply. The difference in tone between the two letters is indicative of the widening gap between rank and file Wobblies and union officials on the issue of how to respond to the war.

DOCUMENT SIX
Letter

Joseph Ratti to Don Sheridan, secretary, and Roy Brown, chairman of LWIU #500

Whitefish, Montana
April 20, 1917

Fellow Workers:

I am up against a tough proposition, and want to get enlightened a little bit on it. It's on account of the flag. The I.W.W. hall is the only place in town that [is being] forced [to] display that flag, a symbol which means slavery and upholding it, and I believe there is going to be trouble about it too. The last two nights our own American flag was nailed in front of the door, and naturally it was taken down.[5]

Advise me, as I am consulting Turner too now, and want your opinion. You know there is a clause in the [IWW] Constitution which reads: Any and all tactics which bring the goods. I am standing pat, and will not fly the flag of any one nation, as we are international in scope.

Hoping you will look at it from my angle, as I would not like to see this branch fall through [from] any ignorance on my part. I believe a stitch in time saves nine.

Boosting and striving for the O.B.U.
I am for Emancipation,

Jos. J. Ratti
Box 641

P.S.: Answer as soon as possible.

IWW Trial Transcript, pp. 13138-9

DOCUMENT SEVEN

Letter

Don Sheridan to Joseph Ratti

Spokane, Wash.
424 Lindelle Block, April 23, 1917

Jos. J. Ratti
Whitefish, Mont.

Fellow Worker

Your letter, and am sending you a receipt book and some *Workers* under separate cover. If you were getting so short, why did you not say so before? I have already sent 50 to Hegge and Miller each.

About the receipts for Hegge and Miller, there were no reports from them the last time you sent yours in. I got a report from Hegge today. For what reports did you want receipts? Note that the soldiers are in Whitefish; they are also at [St.] Maries and Fortine[6]; they are guarding life and property the officers told Turner. It will make it a little more difficult to keep scabs from working. They told him they were not to take sides with anyone. But they are going to post men along the railroad track, and all men would have to halt when the soldiers ordered them to do so.

About the flag now, rather than have a rumpus it will be better to let it stick; let them put it up though, and if you see that it will make trouble, just leave it there. I would rather you kept it down though.

Jim Rowan is down there now, and you may have a visit from him.

With Best Wishes, I am
Yours for Industrial Freedom,
Sec'y Spokane I.W.W.

IWW Trial Transcript, pp. 13201-2

Little and Haywood Move Far Apart

The debate on the IWW's stance toward the war grew increasingly strident as the federal government clamped down on any opposition. This can be seen most clearly in the series of letters exchanged by Frank Little and Bill Haywood. Haywood and Little had developed a close working relationship over many years, and, indeed, Haywood had relied on Little to carry out sensitive missions for the union. Nevertheless, their friendship unraveled as their viewpoints diverged. Indeed, Haywood and Little were on a collision course that was only averted by Little's murder in August 1917.

DOCUMENT EIGHT
Telegram
Frank Little to William Haywood[7]

Jerome, Ariz.
April 10, 1917

Suggest that a conference of all radical organizations be called to propose to fight compulsory enlistment [and] to prepare and advocate the general strike of all industries to strike for industrial freedom of the working class. Must act at once.

DOCUMENT NINE
Letter[8]
Frank Little to William Haywood

April 16th, 1917

William D. Haywood
Chicago, Ill.

Fellow Worker:

I have written several letters since I heard from you, but, as I have been on the road, I suppose there are letters at Miami.

Haven't heard from you since the WAR was declared. But, in looking over *Solidarity*, am unable to decide whether it stands for the worker enlisting in the army or not. It is the duty of the I.W.W. to oppose war at any and all cost. We are opposed to war, and our papers should let the readers know where we stand. The capitalist will try to force our members in the army, and we should let the workers know why they should refuse to serve their enemy. It is true that they may line a few of us up and shoot us. But that must be expected in the fight for freedom. And just at the present it is your fight. I, for one, will go the route for any charge they want to put against me, to help prevent this country (or the workers of this country) going to the front. I sent a wire to *Sol* in plenty of time for this issue giving my view, but it was not published. What in hell are we going to do? Lie down like a bunch of curs and let them force us to war. I, for one, say no. By God Damn I will not keep still. And I want our papers [to] express themselves. If we fight, let us fight for freedom. And now is the time to take a stand.

F. H. Little

DOCUMENT TEN

Letter[9]

William Haywood to Frank Little

April 21, 1917

Frank H. Little
Box 445
Miami, Ariz.

Fellow Worker:

Yours of the 16th received.

I can't help but think that you are making a serious mistake in advocating public statements that will result in nothing else than disbarring our papers from the mail. Already, *Rabochy*, the Russian paper, *A Bermunkas*, the Hungarian paper have been suppressed. Do you want the same thing to happen to the rest of the I.W.W.?

My advice in this hour of crisis is a calm head and cool judgment.

Talk is not the thing needed now. Many of the members feel as you do, but regard the present war between capitalist nations as of small importance when compared with the great Class War in which all are engaged.

Just got a letter from Don Sheridan, secretary-treasurer of No. 500 with check for $500 to apply on account. Other Industrial Unions are moving.

> With Best Wishes, I am
> Yours for Industrial Freedom
> General Secretary-Treasurer

In July 1917, the General Executive Board met in Chicago. It had several contentious issues to discuss, but the most critical was the union's position on the war. Frank Little presented a draft statement that called for militant resistance to the war effort. Haywood rejected the proposed statement, arguing that the adoption of such a statement would guarantee the destruction of the IWW. No decision was reached, and the General Executive Board never agreed on a statement.

A copy of Little's draft statement was seized during the Bureau of Investigation raids on the Chicago headquarters. It was then presented as a prosecution exhibit during the conspiracy trial of 1918.

DOCUMENT ELEVEN

Proposed Statement to the General Executive Board on War[10]
Frank Little [July 1917]

The General Executive Board of the I.W.W., in session assembled, reaffirm with unfaltering determination the unalterable opposition of the Industrial Workers of the World and its membership to all wars, and the participation therein of the membership of the Industrial Workers of the World.

We wish to draw the attention of the membership of the I.W.W. [to] the fact that any member of the Industrial Workers of the World who becomes a member of the military or naval forces of this, or any other country where we organize, cannot retain his membership in this organization.[11]

Members of the I.W.W. who at the outbreak of the European War enlisted in the Canadian forces were summarily expelled from the organization; this action will be strictly followed in all cases.

In this mad chaos of bloodshed and slaughter that has engulfed the world, all the rights we have fought so long and bitterly to retain and enlarge are in danger of being crushed and suppressed by the ruthless powers of Capitalism; therefore it behooves the membership of the I.W.W. to look well to their rights, and to battle for their principles with intensified vigor and courage. We must not allow the masters of industry, under the cloak of "military expediency," or the subtle and hypocritical lie of this being a "war for democracy," to destroy every vestige of our organization, to stifle the voice of the workers, to crush the working-class press, by abrogating the rights of Free Speech, Free press and Free Assemblage, as they are now doing on every hand. These tyrannical acts and usurpation of power, we cannot and shall not tolerate without protest and resistance by all methods within our power; we must let these tyrants understand that they cannot fool us with their "War for Democracy" lies, by destroying Democracy here.

We of the Industrial Workers of the World, who have always opposed war and any participation therein, consider our membership exempt from any participation in this or any other war, just as much as the Quakers or any religious sect that oppose war; we oppose war not from religious motives, but from motives of principle; we abhor war because we abhor murder, rapine and wanton destruction.

We further wish to assure the membership that the entire strength of the organization, morally, economically and financially, will be used to support any of our members in their refusal to kill or be killed.

We wish to serve notice on our capitalist masters that we are just as bitterly opposed to their wars of commercialism today as we ever were; our refusal to endorse or participate in their wars is just as firm today as it ever was. We will resent with all the power at our command any attempt upon their part to compel us, the disinherited, to participate in a war that can only bring in its wake death and untold misery, privation and suffering to millions of workers, and only serve to further rivet the chains of slavery on our necks, and render still more secure the power of the few to control the destinies of the many.

Seeking a Safe Alternative

After Little's murder, the debate within the IWW leadership became far more muted. The IWW looked for a way to maintain a semblance of opposition to the war while avoiding any action that would immediately trigger prosecution by the federal government. The following letter from Haywood to the secretary of the Agricultural Workers' Industrial Union indicates that Haywood hoped to align the union with the People's Council for Democracy and the Terms of Peace.

The People's Council was a loose coalition of progressives and moderate socialists that sought to prod the administration into opening negotiations with Germany for a peace based on the formula of "no annexations, no reparations." As it turned out, the governor of Minnesota, with the covert backing of the federal government, prevented the People's Council from holding a national meeting in Minneapolis, and the organization faded into oblivion soon afterward.

DOCUMENT TWELVE
Letter
William Haywood to Forrest Edwards

August 20th-17

Forrest Edwards
Sec'y Treas. A.W.I.U #400
Minneapolis, Minn.

Fellow Worker:

I enclose a copy of a letter received from Fellow Worker Justus Ebert and clipping accompanying same.

We believe that it would be a good idea for a committee representing the I.W.W. [to] appear before this body, with a view of explaining to them the various outrages perpetrated upon our organization, and asking that they give all publicity to same; in other words, we may be able to use them to advantage in the matter of gaining publicity on these things.

Also, as the A.F. of L. is split on the People's Council, we may be able to drive a nail into their coffin by getting into the swim with them.

While the objects of the People's Council are not the things we are striving for entirely, still their fight against Conscription, and their avowed intention to throw the searchlight of publicity on the lawlessness being practiced in the name of patriotism, will enable us, if we can get their attention, to secure much publicity that will aid in our work of propaganda.

If you are in favor of attending this Convention, we will write you credentials for yourself and two more members of a committee you may designate to authorize you to appear before this body to explain our position.

Trusting you will reply at once and let us know what you think of the proposition.

I remain, with best wishes,
Yours for the O.B.U
Sec'y Treas. I.W.W.

IWW Trial Transcript, pp. 5220-2

Conscription

Once the United States declared war on Germany, President Woodrow Wilson was intent on rapidly dispatching millions of soldiers to France to bolster Allied positions along the Western Front. The War Department soon found that voluntary enlistments could not fill the huge quotas deemed necessary. In May 1917, Congress enacted legislation requiring all men between the ages of twenty-one and thirty-nine to register for the draft, with June 5, 1917, set as registration day.

As unpopular as the war was, the draft was even more unpopular. Workers throughout the Western states were opposed to the war and had no intention of being shipped overseas. IWW branches passed resolutions calling on the Chicago headquarters to organize a coordinated resistance to the draft. Repeatedly, rank and file Wobblies wrote to union officials urging them to utilize the IWW's resources to aid those refusing to register, as well as those refusing to serve when conscripted.

In every case, these calls for action were rebuffed. The Wilson administration realized that the draft was the weakest link in the war effort. The government's drive to mobilize an army of three million men could be derailed, or at least stalled, if opponents of the draft were permitted to exercise their right to dissent, as guaranteed by the First Amendment to the Constitution. Any questioning of the draft, even circulating a petition to Congress to repeal that statute, could trigger prosecution under the Espionage Act.

IWW leaders were well aware of the potential dangers of this perilous situation. They therefore rejected rank and file demands that the IWW organize to oppose conscription, arguing that such acts of resistance made no sense until the union had the power to stop the war through a general strike. Still, the pressure from below, and the vocal efforts of Frank Little, made it difficult to entirely ignore the issue. In July 1917, Ralph Chaplin, as editor of *Solidarity*, wrote an editorial condemning the draft, while leaving resistance at the option of each individual. The editorial urged Wobblies to register for the draft as conscientious objectors on the basis of their total opposition to war.

Once again, the IWW vacillated and floundered, unable to adequately cope with a crisis situation. Left to their own devices, many Wobblies were drafted and served as soldiers on the Western Front, although many others avoided military service through individual acts of resistance. Some IWW members were exempted from service because they failed a physical examination. Others refused to register and disappeared. In a few cases, Wobblies fled to Mexico, which provided a safe haven for draft resisters during World War I.

Notwithstanding the lack of support at the national level, a few branches became involved in local efforts to organize a determined resistance to conscription. These efforts pointed the way to an alternative strategy to the ineffectual stance take by most of those in leadership positions.

Prior to Registration Day

Even before the United States declared war on Germany the IWW had already taken a sharply defined position on the draft. When dozens of lumberjacks met to form a new union in March 1917, it was obvious that the United States would soon enter the war, and, once this occurred, only conscription would enable the federal government to raise the huge army required to defeat Germany and it allies.

Although the minutes of the founding convention of the Lumber Workers' Industrial Union #500 do not provide a detailed account of the debates, the resolution to oppose conscription would have been well received. Most Wobblies opposed the war, and were expecting the union to lead a determined resistance to the draft.

DOCUMENT ONE

Resolution
Minutes of the Founding Convention of the
Lumber Workers' Industrial Union
Held in Spokane, Washington
March 4th to 6th, 1917

Report of Resolutions Committee reads:
Resolution #5, Section 7, favoring a general strike in case of compulsory conscription. Committee concurs; adopted by [the] convention.

IWW Trial Transcript, p. 11216

The Issue Debated

The period following the passage of the Selective Service Act on May 18, 1917, and prior to registration day, June 5, 1917, was marked by a spirited debate within the IWW. It was time to put into practice the militant anti-war resolutions that had been passed with little opposition before April 1917.

A branch of the Oil Workers' Industrial Union #230 in Kansas pressed the union's headquarters to move forcefully in organizing a militant opposition to conscription. The branch secretary, Phineas Eastman, would soon be indicted for violating the Espionage Act and a prime piece of evidence presented by the prosecution was the following resolution.[1]

DOCUMENT TWO

Letter[2]

Phineas Eastman to William Haywood

Augusta, Kans., 5-21-17

Wm D Haywood
Sec. Treas. I.W.W.
Chicago

Fellow Worker:

Enclose [to] you a motion made and carried unanimously here at Business Meeting, May 20, 1917.

Yours for Ind. Freedom,
Phineas Eastman
Br. Sec. 1145

P.S. All members are at sea as to what the members as a whole are going to do in re to conscription. This motion is to help, in a specific way, to get down to action & put a stop to speculation.

Motion made at Business Meeting of Augusts Kas. Branch, May 20, 1917:

All members of the I.W.W. [should] Resist Conscription by refusing to join any band of potential murderers, or by any other effective method deemed advisable. Copies of this motion [to] be sent to Wm D. Haywood, Sec. Treas. I.W.W. and Forrest Edwards, Sec. Treas. A.W.O., with the request that these two officials transmit same, with Dispatch, to all unions of the I.W.W. & Delegates in the field.[3]

The debate within the Lumber Workers' Industrial Union #500 was particularly intense as rank-and-file Wobblies pushed the union to implement the resolution on conscription approved by its founding convention. As secretary of the union, James Rowan was well aware that lumberjacks were overwhelmingly opposed to the draft and were expecting the IWW to lead a collective movement of resistance. Nevertheless, Rowan remained adamant, insisting that the union had to concentrate on organizing at the workplace, while avoiding any organized opposition to the war or the draft.

DOCUMENT THREE

Letter

William Hardy to James Rowan

Sandpoint, Idaho, May 21, 1917

James Rowan
Lindelle Block
Spokane, Washington

Fellow Worker: Enclosed please find check and my report for the week ending May 19th. Things are picking up around here again and most of the members are out on the job. Please let me know what action should be taken in regards to this conscription business? What are the fellow workers in Spokane going to do? Are they going to allow themselves to be dragged off to the field of slaughter to protect the Wall Street despots? Or are they going to show their true spirit and revolt against this tyrannical mandate that has been issued by Wilson, [J.P.] Morgan & Co.[4] It is high time that action should be started. Since our freedom, rights and liberty are to be trampled underneath the rule of the iron heel from a gang of broad cloth despots that have long fattened on our flesh and blood. A stop must be put to them. I am ready to do my bit. Are the rest going to do their duty? Ways and means should be planned to stop these dogs from carrying out their plan. Something has got to be done before it is too late.

Yours for the O.B.U.
William Hardy

IWW Trial Transcript, p. 12666

DOCUMENT FOUR

Letter

James Rowan to William Hardy

>Spokane Washington
>424 Lindelle Block
>May 23, 1917

Wm. Hardy
Sand Point, Idaho

Fellow Worker:

Your letter and report at hand and contents noted. Enclosed you will find the receipts for the same. Please make out the #573 reports separate from the #500 one, if you can possibly find the time.[5]

As regards the conscription law, will say that the General Organization has not taken any definite stand in the matter to our knowledge; will say, however, that the coast bunch, and also the boys here, will refuse to register. Of course, we are not shouting this to the house tops; our main efforts must be centered in the organization of the workers. It is only there that we can ever hope to get enough power to successfully fight an issue of that kind. The only thing at present that this office can suggest is that the individual members refuse to register and that must be optional, as there is nothing in the I.W.W. to prevent them from so doing if they wish to. These things are really a side issue; if we do not have the economic power to dictate our actions, it is of little use to raise a ruction about it. By acting solidly and refusing to register we may be able to get away with it; no doubt, this will be taken up by the General Organization and some line of action decided upon.

>With Best Wishes, I am
>Yours for Industrial Freedom,
>Sec'y Spokane I.W.W.

IWW Trial Transcript, pp. 12667-68

DOCUMENT FIVE

Letter

Joseph Ratti to James Rowan

Whitefish, Mont.
5/26/17

James Rowan
Sec. 500

Fellow Worker:

Received your letter of the 25th, and you tell me I did not send [the] Lewis report to you. I sent you everything he sent me. I wrote to him about it, but, as yet, no answer from him. I am glad to hear you are working on the Hegge case there, and we will know definitely what's up. Yesterday, I went to Kalispell[6] to look up a report that was brought in. Well, here it is. They have a fine hall, very reasonable, and, with a little activity, will surely boom. I met Alex Stevenson, who was on a little trot, but he was not carrying credentials when he got drunk. I talked [to him] and told him [that] a good man, when he fails, gets up and tries again. I finally persuaded him [that] I was right, and I took him up to his room. He said he would try to straighten himself up.

Kalispell is certainly big enough to support that hall, if the members wish to make it a success by cutting out [the] booze. The saloons there are a regular mad house. Micho, the fellow I was telling you about, went back to his camp empty-handed, and broke. It cost him about $75.00 to get the boys drunk, and then they would not scab. (Don't you feel sorry?) The boys are standing pat, but looking it square in the face, something [has] got to be done. The way they figure is this: When the selective conscription comes in to play, they expect a bunch of jacks will flock to the river.

By the way, what am I going to do about registering? The fifth is fast approaching, and we [have] to know what to do. I can beat it myself, but some regular plan of action must be made.

Things are picking up, and expect it to be better in the near future. I am checking myself up good. In fact, [I am making an] inventory of everything, [so], if circumstances arise where I would go to jail, we would have everything in good order. (This registration thing has got my goat.) Boosting for the O.B.U.

>With Best Wishes to All,
>   I am for the Emancipation of the Slaves,
>   Joseph J. Ratti

IWW Transcript, pp. 12676-8

DOCUMENT SIX
Letter
James Rowan to Joseph Ratti

May 28, 1917

Jos. J. Ratti
Whitefish, Mont.

Fellow Worker:

Your letter of the 26th at hand and contents fully noted. There was a report for Lewis [that] came here. Try and find him and get it. His application came in all right. In the meantime, we will enter it as being paid on account, and we will get your other reports entered that way. You issued some supplies to a delegate name of Kennedy and neglected to send a bill in here for the amount; look this up, and send it in. Note that you went to Kalispell and that you like the look of things around there. I am glad to hear that; no doubt, we will be able to get Mont. pretty well on the map this summer. Note also about the slip that Stevenson made; we will give him another chance; no doubt he will hang on to himself this time. Note about the fellow going back to his camp empty handed; that is the dope, the boys are realizing the power of solidarity, and that is the thing that brings home the bacon.

Note also that you are worrying about that conscription bill; well, we cannot give you definite instructions about that and you ought to realize it; we have not heard from Haywood, what stand he is taking on it, and this union cannot at this time give out orders or instructions telling its members how to act in that case. It is an individual proposition and the fellows ought to have the guts to make a stand themselves, without getting advice about it. We [can] come out with some statement if all the other unions do, but at the present, as I explained in my former letter, we cannot come out officially with anything about it.[7] The most of the boys here are going to stay pat and let the other side do the squawking.

There will be many among the scissorbills[8], even, who will not register, and I hardly think that the authorities are going to shove us all in the can; if they do, they will have a real lively bunch on their hands; I realize that some of us may go up against it for awhile alright, but better that then going to the trenches in Europe.

> With Best Wishes, I am
> Yours for the O.B.U.
> Sec'y Industrial Union No. 500 I.W.W.

IWW Transcript, pp. 12678-9

The debate on the question of the union's stance on conscription even extended into the leadership. As a member of the General Executive Board, Richard Brazier wrote Haywood calling on the union to act decisively before registration day. Haywood had already decided that such a strategy was too risky and that the IWW should avoid any agitation around the issue of conscription.

DOCUMENT SEVEN

Letter

Richard Brazier to William Haywood

May 26th, 1917
Room 78 Union Block
Seattle

William D. Haywood
Chicago, Ill.

Fellow Worker:

Say Bill, it seems to me that the organization as a whole is sadly neglecting one important issue, and that is the issue of conscription. As yet, we have taken no organized action upon this issue, and it is time something was done. We should take a definite stand upon the question of registration for the draft; we should issue an official announcement that we will resist the enforcement of conscription. I think, myself, that we should register, as that does not bind us to anything, and if the radicals refuse to register they will simply gather them in, and probably intern them, which would smash the movement, but we can register our conscientious objections to the draft and war, if we register, and we can issue an official proclamation that we will resist conscription; there is enough of a sentiment against conscription in this country, if it can only be organized and crystallized to make our protest a real menace to the powers that be. I have in mind a letter to the President of this country from the G.E.B. and yourself [stating] our official position on the draft and war. We can show that as members of the I.W.W. we are denied citizenship in this land. We are practically aliens, and, as such even under own law, cannot be drafted. We can point to the numerous outrages perpetrated upon our members as evidence of the fact that this country [that] they wish us to fight for has denied us even an elementary measure of justice. We can enumerate at length our rooted aversion to all war, whether offensive or defensive. I enclose a brief copy of what I mean. This can be changed by you or Harrison George, or some more capable writer than myself. My idea is to take a bold stand. I am confident [that] we can secure unlimited support. In fact, I have an idea they [opponents of the war] are waiting for the I.W.W. to lead the way.

I enclose my bill for the week. Got your wire re the Montana cases. [I] cannot understand how Miller's case affects the others. If they desire a new trial, and Miller does not, that should not prevent us from doing what we can for the other boys. Let me know [the] full details as soon as you can.

Hoping to Hear from You Soon,
Yours for the O.B.U.
Richard Brazier

IWW Trial Transcript, p. 18789-91

DOCUMENT EIGHT

Statement

Richard Brazier

Enclosure: Proposed Letter to the President

Woodrow Wilson
White House
Washington, D.C.

Honorable Mr. President:

We, the General Executive Board and the Secretary-Treasurer of the Industrial Workers of the World, fearing that you are not in close enough touch with the vast working class to understand or appreciate their bitter sentiments of hostility against the undemocratic, liberty-destroying, militaristic measures which you have been instrumental in fostering, and forcing upon unwilling millions, and feeling that you have been misled by the empty words of false labor leaders, who have been assuring you that the working class supports your "Prussian" militaristic plan of compulsory conscription, which would drive [us] headlong into that whirling of insane carnage and slaughter-the

European war; hundreds of thousands of men who hate the very name of war wish you [to] know that.

It is idle to prate to us about a war for liberty. The war for liberty must be fought in the United States against the enemy within, not upon the blood-stained fields of Flanders, against poor deluded workers who know not what they are fighting for.

We, the members of the Industrial Workers of the World, have been denied the rights of citizenship in this country, which we are now asked to shed our life blood for. We have been treated as aliens, and, as such according to our own laws, are exempt from the draft, from compulsory conscription. [Thus], we are exempt from the hideous crime of slaughtering our fellow men.

Members of the Industrial Workers of the World have been judicially murdered in this land, with not a protest from you, who should be the first to protest. Others are rotting their lives away in dungeons and cells in your jails and penitentiaries, simply because they tried to better the lot of their fellow workers.

The grass is hardly green upon the graves of our dead, who were shot wantonly, with malice aforethought, by officers of the law, aided by the so-called law and order citizens, and not one of them yet brought to book, and [yet] you and the powers that be that are talking about a war of justice: What have you done to get justice for us and ours?

We wish to inform you that we are unutterably opposed to conscription in any form; we wish to inform [you] that we are opposed to all war; we wish to inform you that we will refuse to help build up a military machine that will be used to drive us back to our hovels when we dare to strike for more to eat, or for more of the good things of life. We do not believe that you can destroy Prussian militarism by building up a militarism more ruthless and powerful than the one you seek to destroy. We do not believe you are sincere when say you are waging war for starving Belgium, because if the sight of starving Belgians thousands of miles away arouses your indignation so much that you are willing to send the flower of American manhood to die on [the] fields of Flanders to succor and aid them, [then] why is it that the sight of hungry millions at your own gate arouses no such feelings of indignation?

We refuse to be moved by your sophistry. We refuse to fight for a cause that is tainted with the blood-stained dollars of financial pirates.

We wish to inform you that the membership of the I.W.W., hundreds of thousands strong, together with their sympathizers, and all others who hate war and all its attendant evils, and who love peace and liberty, and who harbor no thoughts of hatred to their fellow man, will resist to the last any and all efforts to conscript us in a war that means nothing to us, [and] that cannot better our economic conditions one iota, but will only place upon us the yoke of military autocracy.

We have the courage to tell you, Mr. President, where we stand. We are workers who are part of the working class, not labor leaders who are so far apart from the workers as [are] the [two] poles.

We hope you will take this message to heart. We hope you will realize that, in the name of liberty, you are destroying every vestige of liberty the American people ever had. Conscription, censorship, suppression of free speech and free press, all in the name of liberty. Mr. President, the gods are laughing.

Yours for Real Democracy and Industrial Freedom

P.S.: Bill, the above letter is only a sample of what I mean, but you get my idea. You must have something like this drawn up, and send it to Wilson, not that he will ever get it, but we can say it was sent. You can have it printed in our papers as the official stand of the I.W.W. upon this damned conscription. Of course, I am not asking that you print the above, for this is only my idea of what should be done.

R.B.

IWW Trial Transcript, pp. 18794-97

DOCUMENT NINE

Letter

William Haywood to Richard Brazier

June 4th, 1917

Richard Brazier
78 Union Block
Seattle, Washington

Fellow Worker:

Yours of the 26th inst., with bill for $22.70, is received. Enclosed find check for the amount.

Have carefully read the open letter which you enclose. Have received several suggestions of a like nature, but have not deemed it advisable to act upon them. Strange to me that up to date not a line has been received from any source suggesting what might be said to the membership, but I feel pretty well satisfied as to what the general thought is, and what the general action will be. The time, in my opinion, has not yet arrived to impress upon the public stronger than we have already done.

Got your telegram, and have been awaiting results, or developments rather, at Kansas City. The last information that I got from there, no charges had been preferred against Gilday, and a trial committee had not yet been elected. Before I got this word from Lambert, got a telegram from Forrest Edwards saying that the convention had instructed him to telegraph me that Ettor was wanted there in Gilday's defense. Thinking, of course, that the trial was on, I telegraphed fifty dollars to Ettor. I regretted it later, when I received Lambert's letter, for I knew then that the constitutional requirements had not been complied with. I have not forwarded the letter received from you while on the Range to K.C. Will not do so until they are needed for the trial, if there is to be one.

If Gilday is now trying to fasten something upon some member of the General Executive Board, it is the first big piece of detective work that he has done.

In regard to 573, I consider it very important that an office be established for the Construction Workers at Seattle. This is one demand of 382 that should be conceded without question. On the proposition of an industrial union giving a sub to every member, 573 made a serious mistake [since] the old executive, the Convention and the new executive board went on record in favor of a sub from some I.W.W. paper to every new member. This, you will remember, was embodied in my report, which was adopted by the Convention. I have been hammering at this proposition ever since the Convention adjourned. The papers are the greatest educational factor that we have in the Organization. The *Industrial Worker* and *Solidarity* should each have now at least 35,000 subs. Keep working on this proposition of subs for new members. It must be uniformly adopted.

>With best wishes, I am
>Yours for Industrial Freedom
>General Secretary-Treasurer

IWW Trial Transcript, pp. 18791-3

Resistance

In spite of the lack of support from general headquarters, in several communities where the IWW had developed deep roots the union participated in an organized effort to defeat the draft. Butte, Montana was the stronghold of copper miners, a city with a long history of radical politics. On registration day, June 5, 1917, hundreds of miners joined a march protesting the war and the draft organized by the IWW branch and a group of Irish radicals. The march was dispersed at the point of bayonets by federal troops sent to Butte for that very purpose. The following leaflet was distributed in the days leading up to the demonstration.

DOCUMENT TEN

Leaflet

Unsigned but Distributed by Butte I.W.W. and the
Pearse-Connolly Club of Butte[9]
[June 4, 1917]

WAR IS HELL, WE DO NOT WANT IT

On June 5th we are ordered to register that we may be examined as to our fitness to kill and murder workingmen of other countries against whom we have no grievance. We will be sent to war, to pillage, destroy, murder and burn; to lay waste fertile fields and homes; to break the hearts of gray-haired mothers and fathers, happy, laughing sisters and sweethearts; to make fatherless and homeless hundreds of thousands of beautiful, innocent, big-eyed babies. We must leave behind us everything a man holds dear in order that we may more efficiently butcher other workingmen and torture and starve their families.

We have been taught that our land is the "Cradle of Freedom"; that our rights and liberties would be protected and defended; yet we are, at the behest of the money powers, to be taken forcibly to kill and be killed. We are to be forced to assist the nation which has riveted the chains of slavery around Ireland, and which is at this moment forging fast the fetters of bondage for millions of Hindus, and scheming to break the power of the people of Russia.

They say that in order to destroy the militarism of Germany it is necessary to create a militarism in this country that will be far more terrible than Germany's, and to that end they levy a tax greater by far than the world has ever known.

Were the American people consulted about this war? Were we given a chance to express our opinions? Who wants this war? Ninety per cent of the American people are against this war. The only support for war comes from the moneyed interests in general, who will make enormous profits from war. The newspapers belong to these people, and reflect only their opinions.

Who parades when there is a demonstration held? Old men, women and children, the Chamber of Commerce, and men who would not volunteer when they were asked to.

We are facing a world crisis. Can the American nation be forced to war against the will of its people? Our fathers fought against militarism and compulsory training. We were not plunged into war until AFTER [THE] ELECTION, and if an election were due to be held in one year, we would not be at war now.

Who will fight this war? Workingmen! What have we at stake? Nothing! The money powers are already preparing to import a million Chinamen to take our places.[10]

STRIKE AGAINST MILITARISM

STRIKE AGAINST WAR

DO NOT REGISTER TOMORROW.
Let those who want war register.

STAY AT HOME.
Thousands of workingmen have refused to register.

Mothers, DON'T LET your sons become cannon fodder.
THINK what they mean to you.

Wives, DON'T LET your husbands go from your side.

Men, THINK of the duty you owe to Civilization. DON'T REGISTER. Rather die at home, defending the rights and peace of the World's people, than be forced to murder and death in the blood-soaked trenches of Europe. A silent strike against war means the greatest step ever taken by the American working class.

DO YOUR SHARE. DON'T REGISTER.

DOWN WITH MILITARISM. DOWN WITH WAR PROFITEERS.

DOWN WITH INVISIBLE GOVERNMENT

IWW Trial Transcript, pp. 16511-13

In northern Minnesota, the union had established a solid base of support among Finnish iron ore miners. Opposition to the war and the draft was deeply felt in this community. IWW activists joined with other radicals in hiding draft resisters, even moving them to safer locations. At the same time, activists continue to distribute literature denouncing the war and the draft. The Finnish Wobblies, as well as the Butte miners, demonstrated to the entire union what could have, and should have, been done to build a militant movement to resist the draft.

Charles Jacobson, the secretary-treasurer of the Metal Mine Workers' Industrial Union #490[11], ordered the posting of two hundred copies of the following flyer:

DOCUMENT ELEVEN
Letter to *Solidarity*

June 9th, 1917

Solidarity
1001 W. Madison St.
Chicago, Ill.

Fellow Workers:

Set a little of this in the next *Solidarity*.

The new conscription law that has gone into effect lately seems to be working fine on the Mesaba range. This conscription law has put the fear of [the] lord into the workers in the entire iron industry and [they] are linging [joining] by the hundreds every week.

Not since the strike of last summer has the Metal Mine Workers' Industrial Union increased its membership as fast as it has in the last two weeks.

On registration day, there were men always waiting for their chance to get the little red card. Early in the morning, two men came to the hall and asked the janitor if this was the place where they could register. The janitor, Mrs. Johnson said, "Yes, Fellow Worker Jacobson is registering into the I.W.W., if that is what you mean. Go ahead upstairs and you will be next." These men turned black in the face and went out, without registering that day, but since [then they] have registered into the I.W.W.

Registration day seems as if it was a failure on the Mesaba range. In Virginia,[12] there were supposed to be some 4 or 5000 men between the ages of 21 and 30, and only 1800 registered and were ready to go to war. There were arrests made every day of the so called slackers, but the miners are going to stop the entire iron industry if the men that are in jail are not released. So, the bosses on the range are in a bad mixup at the present time.

The other new law that was made especially for the I.W.W. Is being put into practice. Three fellow workers were jailed and charges made that they have violated the new syndicalism law. The men were found sticking up stickerettes, and that is advocating sabotage.

With Best Wishes,
Yours for the O.B.U.

IWW Trial Transcript, 12229

Jacobson also ordered the posting of two hundred copies of the following flyer:

DOCUMENT TWELVE
Circular Statement[13]

June 22, 1917

Workers in the Iron Industry:

Your attention is called to the fact that in the Land of Liberty, the home of the free, hundreds of our fellow workers have been arrested, and thrown into jails that the workers have built, for the reason that they did not register, because they knew that the Constitution of the United States does not allow any force to be practiced on any man under the jurisdiction of the United States, and because they do not believe in wars, and practicing [the] killing [of] their fellow men for the benefit of [the] few over-fed parasites, while they themselves are in urgent need of the necessities of life.

You fellow workers think this over for a minute in your head, and you will soon see that if we workers do not help ourselves, the master class will not help us. We are here producing the iron of which the war machineries are built from. Thousands of tons of our sweat and blood are sunk into the bottoms of the oceans, and millions of our fellow men are being killed, and others are wounded for cannon food.

You workers must stop furnishing the master the material of which the war structures are made of, and [at the] same time defend our innocent fellow workers, who believe that they will not murder your brothers or your father, nor destroy your home.

We appeal to you workers of the iron industry to prepare for a walk out from your jobs, and demand that the imprisoned fellow workers are immediately released. Thousands of men in the copper industries in the state of Montana are on strike already to defend our fellow workers; thousands more will in [a] few days be out in the lumber industry of the West.

Prepare yourselves miners and all other workers to go out on strike on the moment's notice. DO NOT BE SLACKERS TO DEFEND YOUR OWN CLASS.

Even after registration day, the debate on conscription continued within the IWW. Harry Green was a Wobbly activist and migrant farm worker. He wrote to Spokane, the regional office for IWW unions in the region, including the Agricultural Industrial Workers' Union #400.

DOCUMENT THIRTEEN

Letter

Harry Green to Don Sheridan

Arnegard, N. Dak.
6-23-17

Don Sheridan
Spokane, Wash.

Fellow Worker:

Enclosed find card & 5 $ bill. Stamp same up to end of Aug. 8 months.

Send me single back copies of *Sol* and the *Worker* as far back as you like, as I have not seen a copy since Xmas. Also, a copy of *Patriotism and the Worker, Crime and Criminals* and any new dope that you have that is good propaganda.

I jimmed my foot this last winter [and] was laid up for several months. Owing to lack of coin, I was unable to choose my job or its location. I worked for the toughest character that exists, and although it is against my principle to quit a bum job, or a hostile driver, I had to do it.

I left him in the lurch, and he refused to settle up. I needed the mon', and right badly, so I was forced to visit a shyster lawyer. We got the money. The shyster needed his too. Anyhow, the harvest days are near and the kitty needs milk. I'm absolutely disgusted with this life on the farm, especially in this scissorbill locality. It's the greatest cousin outfit I've struck.

I was in a quandary as to whether to register on June 5th knowing that the law exists on account of those who respect same, and not greatly fearing the 1 year in the can, [so] it was pretty hard for me to obey Fellow Worker Wilson's orders. I subject myself to correction as I became faithful to his mandate and registered.

The scissor I am working for was very enthusiastic over the President's call, and brother of same was the registerer. He asked me whether I had any reasons for exemption or objection to [the] draft. I said yes, conscientious objections to enlist to kill my brothers of any country, or those in the U.S.A.

I'd like to know the stand taken by the membership at large in the O.B.U. I really think it would have been good policy to register [as conscientious objectors] just to let the parasites know that there is some who have the intelligence enough to refuse to do their dirty work, but I suppose the best policy would be to ignore them and refuse to register. I had no time to ascertain the stand of the I.W.W. in this matter as I was ignorant of the [Selective Service] bill until a few days before registration day. I realize that it is very poor policy to render information and jeopardize oneself in so paltry an affair.

I heard a report that the President has ordered sittings of judges in the near future to hear and decide whether individuals have (just?) reasons for exemption. What are we to do? Remain neutral till they start to draft, or go up and tell that old fossilized judge that we are international slaves? I guess this scissor bill community has effected my think tank, as I have lost all initiative; so if there is any life up there, call me as I need some education as to what a rebel consists of.

I have raised the anger of both slaves and bosses here as to my views regarding the war and U.S. intervention. I realize that I am a damn fool to try to enlighten such bone heads, or to remain in such a community when there is work to be done for the malcontents in other places, but I've been so (blessed) with lack of coin and back-bone that I choose same rather than suffer affliction elsewhere. I think I'm about foot-loose to travel any time I am assured of a bum job and a discontented bunch of slaves. Maybe I am asking too much, but if you can inform me, do so, but don't steer me into a secretary job in a wobbly local (nuf said). Well, I guess I'll ring off as I realize that I've said nothing, and done nothing, and that leaves nothing, so good-bye and best wishes to the O.B.U.

> I remain yours for Internationalism and Freedom
> Harry Green 899

P.S. If the waste paper basket is the place for this, let her go. I'm willing. (How much did you subscribe to liberty issue?) I'm writing Edwards, so if he has requested information as to my whereabouts, he'll soon learn that I'm not in the trenches of capitalists or capitalism. If there should happen to be an over payment, and you cannot supply me with said literature to cover enclosed surplus cash, use it for the cause.

IWW Trial Transcript, pp. 13229-32

DOCUMENT FOURTEEN

Letter

James Rowan[14] to Harry Green

June 28, 1917

Harry Green
Arenegard, N. Dak.

Fellow Worker:

Your letter of the 23rd at hand and contents fully noted. Enclosed you will find the dues book with the stamps and the papers on hand. Will send you some of the latest issues so you will get some of the news.

Note about your misfortune in getting your foot jammed, but, as you say, the harvest days are near and the kitty must be fed.

Note that Fellow Worker Wilson's proclamation put you in somewhat of a quandary about the correct position for a rebel to take. However, you did not violate any principle by registering, as most of the wobblies who were of age did the same. No use filling all the jails in the country for we can do more good on the outside. No official stand has been taken by the I.W.W. on this. It was left to the judgment of the individual members.

There is plenty of work of all kinds for all rebels who understand something of the class struggle, and you will find it out as soon as you leave your rusticated surroundings.

We have a big strike of the lumber workers on our hands in the district, and it bids fair to develop into a real general strike. All the strikers are attending to business in great style, and are getting ready for the struggle. All the camps and most of the mills are tied up tight. The Seattle district, where they have been organizing to beat the band the last few months, may join the strike after the 4th. The situation looks good, and the strikers have great confidence in the union, and are showing a fine sense of solidarity.

> With Best Wishes, I am
> Yours for the O.B.U.
> Sec'y Industrial Union No. 500 I.W.W.

IWW Trial Transcript. pp. 13232-3

Seeking a Middle Ground

At its July 1917 meeting, the General Executive Board reached an impasse as it attempted to reach an agreement on the stance to be taken by the union on conscription. Frustrated by the GEB's failure to reach a decision, Ralph Chaplin, as editor of *Solidarity*, wrote an editorial that attempted to present a position that would satisfy both sides.

With this editorial the IWW sought to claim a middle ground, stating its opposition to the draft, while leaving the issue in the hands of each individual Wobbly. Nevertheless, federal prosecutors cited this editorial as evidence that the union had deliberately violated the Espionage Act by obstructing the draft. On the other hand, Chaplin's position presented an entirely individualistic answer to a critical problem confronting the entire organization. Each member was left on his own to confront the Selective Service System. Furthermore, the specific proposal advanced by Chaplin was bound to fail, since the government categorically rejected every claim for conscientious objector status that was not rooted in religious pacifist convictions.

DOCUMENT FIFTEEN

Ralph Chaplin, Editorial in *Solidarity*
July 28, 1917

WERE YOU DRAFTED?

Where the I.W.W. Stands on the Question of War:

The attitude of the Industrial Workers of the World is well known to the people of the United States and is generally recognized by the labor movement throughout the world.

Since its inception, our organization has opposed all national and imperialistic wars. We have proved, beyond the shadow of a doubt, that war is a question with which we never have and never intend to compromise.

Members joining the military forces of any nation have always been expelled from the organization.

The I.W.W. has placed itself on record regarding its opposition to war, and also as being bitterly opposed to having its members forced into the bloody and needless quarrels of the ruling class of different nations.

The principle of the international solidarity of labor to which we have always adhered makes it impossible for us to participate in any and all of the plunder-squabbles of the parasite class.

Our songs, our literature, the sentiment of the entire membership-the very spirit of our union, give evidence of our unalterable opposition to both capitalism and its wars.

All members of the I.W.W. who have been drafted should mark their claims for exemption 'I.W.W.: opposed to war.'

Confronting Repression

From its formation in 1905, the IWW organizers were subjected to harassment and brutality. As radicals committed to the overthrow of the capitalist system, the union made an obvious target. At first, repressive measures were primarily undertaken by private detective agencies in the employ of large corporations. Gunmen were hired to assault Wobbly organizers, while the union was penetrated by informants. The IWW responded by attempting to expose the informants in its midst.

The IWW was also targeted by local authorities who, under pressure from business interests, tried to squelch the union's organizing drives in their localities. The result was a series of free speech fights as the IWW organized mass protests to defend its constitutional right to hold public rallies. In general, the union succeeded in reversing local statutes banning peaceful assemblies.

Thus, the union was able to overcome repression during its first decade. The union remained intact and slowly growing. These early successes gave the IWW the spurious hope that the commitment and militancy of its members would inevitably guarantee the defeat of every effort to crush it. This was a dangerous illusion.

World War I significantly altered the overall context. As the union maintained its anti-militarist stance, as it continued to organize militant strikes, the authorities in Western states began to consider the IWW as a serious threat. In early 1917, several states started enacting legislation banning criminal syndicalism, thus rendering the union an illegal organization. Wobblies began receiving lengthy prison sentences for violating these statutes, as the level of repression was ratcheted upward.

When the United States declared war on Germany in April 1917, the IWW confronted a threat to its continued existence. The passage of the Espionage Act in June 1917, with its provision of up to twenty year jail sentences for those who disrupted the war effort, provided the federal government with the authority to destroy those it targeted.

As the summer of 1917 unfolded, it became increasingly clear that the federal government was preparing to prosecute the union. The Chicago headquarters came under intensive and intrusive surveillance. Leaks to friendly journalists made it clear that the Department of Justice would soon seek indictments. The union had to prepare for the worst.

Unfortunately, the IWW failed to adequately respond to this crisis situation. In part, this was because the union prided itself on being an open, transparent organization and thus was unwilling to establish secretive organizational structures. Wobbly leaders were also convinced that repression could be deflected and that a successful legal defense could be organized. Although the General Executive Board attempted to address the crisis, in reality little was done to effectively defend against the coming onslaught.

On September 5, 1917, agents of the Bureau of Investigation raided IWW halls around the country. Similar raids continued for several months, leading to the arrest of nearly two hundred IWW leaders on felony charges of violating the Espionage Act. The IWW was battered, as a coordinated assault left the union in a shambles.

The question remains as to whether the union could have done more to effectively counter the government's attacks.

Private Detectives

From the time of its formation, powerful corporations paid private detective agencies to send informants into IWW branches. The IWW responded by trying to acquire inside information giving the names of informants who could then be publicly exposed and isolated.

The organizing drive aimed at Arizona's copper miners was of critical importance to the union. Mining companies hired numerous informants from several detective agencies in a concerted effort to disrupt the drive. Vincent St. John, who had resigned as General Secretary-Treasurer to become a prospector in New Mexico, offered to help by creating a phony company as cover. He then requested reports from detective agencies by posing as an employer worried that the IWW would seek to organize his workforce.

The following documents show Haywood passing on information he had received from St. John to Grover Perry, the secretary of the Metal Mine Workers' Union #800. Haywood also provided St. John with bogus letterhead stationary so that St. John could successfully claim to be the owner of a mining company. It is not clear from the few documents placed in the trial transcript relating to this venture whether St. John was actually able to acquire information that enabled the union to expose informants within its ranks. In any case, the private detective agencies were quite successful in placing informants in influential positions in key branches of the IWW.

DOCUMENT ONE

Letter

William Haywood to Grover Perry

Chicago, Ill. Feb. 3, 1917

Grover H. Perry
General Delivery
Phoenix, Arizona

Fellow Worker:

Enclosed please find check $25.00 on account of wages.
With best wishes, I am
Yours for Industrial Freedom,
Wm. D. Haywood
General Sec'y-Treas.

P.S.: Got a letter from the Saint with a document showing that the mining companies of Arizona are paying considerable attention to the I.W.W. It seems that there is a Pinkerton in the W.F.M. office that is furnishing this agency with everything that goes through there, so it will stand you in good stead to be careful of all strangers. I am sending you $100.00 by wire.

Bill

IWW Transcript, p. 8507

DOCUMENT TWO

Letter

William Haywood to Vincent St. John

April 4th, 1917

Vincent St. John
Jicarilla, New Mex.

Fellow Worker:

By even[ing] mail I am sending you letterheads which I have had printed, and which I note you will use to get in touch with some of the 'fink' agencies, and learn first hand just what they contemplate doing against the I.W.W.

Excuse delay in responding to your letter. I had put it away in a pigeon-hole, and just came across it tonight. Jack Farley has just called me up to give some word to one or two of the boys about a meeting of the stockholders. Jack has been working like a Trojan here, and has, I think been fairly successful.

Enclosed find copies of 'Dutch Love' as requested.

With Best Wishes, I am

Yours for Industrial Freedom,

General Secretary-Treasurer

IWW Trial Transcript, pp. 10762-3

Criminal Syndicalism

Until 1917, government repression of the IWW had been restricted to the local level, where ordinances were enacted restricting the right of the union to hold public rallies. In March 1917, the state of Idaho approved legislation making it illegal to advocate sabotage, or the destruction of private property, with the intent of bringing about social change. Similar legislation was soon passed in several other Western states. Criminal syndicalism laws specifically targeted the IWW. Courts ruled that an IWW member who carried a copy of the little red song book could be prosecuted for advocating sabotage since one of the songs, Joe Hill's Casey Jones, humorously referred to the derailing of a locomotive during a strike.

The following document written at a time when criminal syndicalism laws were first being passed, indicates that Haywood was convinced that the union would be able to easily overcome the impact of these laws. This sense of riding the tide toward an inevitable victory was one reason that the IWW failed to cope with the ruthless repression it confronted in 1917.

DOCUMENT THREE

Letter

William Haywood to Don Sheridan

Chicago, Ill., March 10, 1917

Don Sheridan
421 Lindelle Block
Spokane, Wash.

Fellow Worker:

Yours of the 6th instant, with $12.50 donation to the German paper, is received. Enclosed find receipt for the amount.

Got a copy of the bill introduced in the Senate of the state of Washington. While I recognize that the measure is directed against the I.W.W., the foolish legislators do not realize that the Industrial Workers of the

World is neither a criminal nor a syndicalist organization. By the way, union branches are growing in that section of the country; our membership will be so strong that laws of that kind will have little effect.

Before attempting to express an opinion about [how] the supplies that you have on hand could be divided up, will first want information as to how, and to what branch, supplies are charged.[1] If the supplies that have been sent to you have been used indiscriminately [by] the members of #400, #573, Lumber Workers and others, it is going to be a difficult proposition to allot them.

That is, if Lumber Workers #500 [having] started feel that they have any interest in the supplies on hand. It would seem to me, without having any definite knowledge of the situation, and the accounts of [the] Lumber Workers and [the] Agricultural Workers have not been kept separate, the better thing is to turn all of the supplies on hand over to Spokane Branch Agricultural Workers #400.

Perhaps an agreeable understanding can be arrived at and a part of the money you have on hand can be left in the treasury of [the] Lumber Workers Union #500. In effecting a satisfactory settlement such a mixup is concerned, it wants to be approached in a spirit of fairness, a sense of justice, and the realization that wherever the money goes it will be used to build up the Industrial Workers of the World.

It may be best to turn all of the money over to #400, [the] starting [supplies for] Lumber Workers Industrial Union #500 can be credited to the account of Agricultural Workers #400, and charged to the account of Lumber Workers Industrial Union #500. In your financial report, I see no division in the accounts of #400 and the Lumber Workers, in which event the pro rata proposition would be the best solution.

Tell Gurley Flynn that I received a personal letter fro Fred Hestlewood.

    With Best Wishes, I am
    Yours for Industrial Freedom
    Wm. D. Haywood,
    General Secty-Treas.

IWW Trial Transcript, pp. 11295-97

Even after the United States had declared war on Germany, the IWW still clung to the illusion that it could not be defeated and that the defeat of the capitalist system was inevitable. This mistaken bravado underpins the following editorial from the union's most important newspaper.

DOCUMENT FOUR

Editorial
April 21, 1917
Solidarity

THE IRRESISTIBLE IWW

The IWW is on the ascendancy. Capitalism is on the decline. Nothing on earth can stop the one from growing or the other from disintegrating. Social and industrial changes are as inevitable as seasonal changes as irresistible as the sunrise. The world has outgrown Capitalism, and Industrial Democracy is the next step in human progress. At the present time, with greed and blood-lust rampant, and the whole world being turned into a shambles, the industrialist is the only one remaining calm and clearsighted-the only one uninfected with hysteria of any kind. Why should we excite ourselves over the noise Capitalism makes in digging its own grave?

The blood-blinded plutocrats are trying to prolong the life of Capitalism as long as possible. They would like to perpetuate their iron sway for all time; to breed more predatory parasites on one hand and more docile slaves on the other-indefinitely. But this is a dream from which they will be rudely awakened. It is not we who will destroy them, but they who are destroying themselves. Karl Marx said that Capitalism came into the world reeking blood and dirt at every pore, and it appears it will leave the world the same way. It will then be up to the Industrial Unions of the IWW to build up the New Society from the wreck and ruin of the old.

But the IWW will succeed, no matter what happens in the near future. If unmolested, it will continue its vigorous growth with unprecedented rapidity, or it will thrive prodigiously on persecution. The IWW does not depend on the guidance of "leaders"; it has none-each member is a "leader"– and they can't all be thrown in jail at the same time. The IWW is an industrial army in which every private is an officer, every officer a private, every member a recruiting sergeant. Arrest an organizer and a hundred more fall in line to take his place; deport a job delegate and a dozen are left behind; drive a speaker from the street or lecture hall and the incessant organization in the industries is augmented just that much; arrest one editor and any number of others are at hand who can do the work of editing as well or better; stop the distribution of IWW papers and they will be distributed underground, as was done in Russia until Industrial Autocracy is [was] also forced to its doom; level the entire organization to the ground and it will grow back stronger than ever. The One Big Union is indestructible. The inexorable laws of history cannot be stopped with bullets nor legal mandates. The IWW is here to stay.

Preparing for the Worst

By the summer of 1917, union leaders realized that the federal government was preparing to initiate a coordinated campaign of repression with the explicit goal of destroying the union as a credible threat. When the General Executive Board met in Chicago in mid-July 1917, the issue of the union's stance toward the war was the foremost topic. Although the GEB failed to reach a decision on this crucial issue, the minutes of the meeting note two other decisions that were made.

First, the GEB approved a list of substitutes for those serving in key posts. This made sense as a defensive strategy, but recording the list did not. Bureau of Investigation agents discovered the minutes during their raids on the union's headquarters and made sure that every Wobbly leader on the list of alternates was indicted and jailed.

Second, the GEB mandated Haywood to deposit $10,000 in a safe deposit box in a reliable bank. This was a sizable sum in 1917, roughly equivalent to $200,000 in current dollars. There is no indication in the transcript of where this sum of money went; perhaps it was used to pay the many attorneys involved in the defense of the IWW leadership during the Chicago conspiracy trial. There is also the question of where this cash came from. The IWW was growing rapidly during the

"The Unconquerables"

Leland Chumley
Solidarity
October 20, 1917

summer of 1917, but it is still highly unlikely that the union would have $10,000 in cash stashed away at its general headquarters. The government did audit the IWW accounting books, but the origin of large sums recorded as assets was not specified. It is possible that the IWW had a large donor who did not wish to be known.

DOCUMENT FIVE

Minutes of the General Executive Board
Afternoon Session, July 4, 1917

Moved by Wiertola, sec. by Lambert. That substitute General Secretary-Treasurer and Substitute General Executive Board Members be appointed to take office, in case of any emergency, until such time as regular officers are elected and installed. Carried.

Substitutes for General Secretary-Treasurer:

E.F. Doree. Grover Perry. W.T. Nef. Herbert Mahler. Vincent St. John.

Substitutes for General Executive Board Members:

Substitutes for Richard Brazier: J.I. Turner. James Rowan.

Substitutes for C.L. Lambert: Herbert Mahler; Ted Fraser.

Substitutes for Wm. Wiertola: Steve Holso; Frank Westerlund.

Substitutes for F.H. Little: Joe Oates, Chas. McWhirt.

Substitutes for Francis Miller: Gildo Mazarella; Ignacius Logis.

Moved by Lambert, sec. By Brazier, that the Secretary-Treasurer be instructed to put away an amount of up to $10,000 (bills) in a safety deposit vault in some reliable banking house. Substitute Secretarys to be furnished with the information necessary to secure a key to the safety deposit vault when it comes their turn to serve as substitute secretary. Carried.

Wm. Wiertola   C.L. Lambert
F.H. Little   Francis Miller
Richard Brazier

IWW Trial Transcript, pp. 10769-70

Quashing the Lumberjacks' Strike

By July 1917, the Arizona strike of copper miners had been crushed, but the walkout of lumberjacks throughout the Pacific Northwest continued. The federal government viewed the strike as a significant threat to the war effort, and thus escalated its pressure on the strikers. IWW activists were detained and union halls were closed throughout the region. At the same time, governors of the states involved began coordinating their efforts to break the strike.

As secretary of the Lumber Workers' Industrial Union, James Rowan could see the morale of the strikers was beginning to falter. Furthermore, Rowan understood that his office in Spokane, Washington would soon be closed. Nevertheless, the following letter from Rowan to Peter Green, the secretary of the Portland branch of the LWIU, indicates that Rowan had still not formulated a meaningful response to the campaign of repression.

DOCUMENT SIX
Letter
James Rowan to Peter Green

July 14, 1917

Peter A. Green
Portland, Oregon

Fellow Worker:

Your last two letters at hand and contents carefully read. Note that you decided to abandon the bulletin and the district organizations for the time being. Alright, it will be best under the circumstances.

Things are certainly happening here. They have closed up the halls at Bushers Ferry, St. Maries, La Grande, Pasco, N. Yakima, and the delegate has quit at Ellensburg, just in time, I guess.[2] There are [so] many under arrest that we have lost track of them. We are having a hot time alright. It will only be a matter of a few days till the office is also closed, and we have made preparations accordingly.

Still, the situation is not so bad; the coast has commenced to come out, and we will hit the lumber trust one good wallop anyway. The strikers here are still on the job, though, of course, some of them are getting weak-kneed.

The papers here have been fierce for the last few days, and the governors of Idaho and Wash. had a meeting to discuss the I.W.W. menace, and see if they could not stop us.[3] They decided that the office had to be closed, so you see we had better get some preparations made.

In case this office is closed, you will have to carry on the work of organization the best you know how. We will inform you where to send mail as soon as possible.

We may get the agriculture workers out on strike as soon as the time is ripe, and may even succeed in getting the miners of the Couer D'Alene[4] out also. We will have to do something decisive, or we will be closed up altogether. In the meantime, we have just begun to fight and we can go some yet.

    Yours for the O.B.U,
      Sec'y Industrial Union No. 500 I.W.W.

IWW Trial Transcript, pp. 13820-21

The Aftermath

The mass arrests that began in September 1917 left the IWW in total disarray. For months, the union devoted all of its energy and resources into defending the dozens of Wobblies who had been jailed by state and federal authorities.

At first, the union attempted to maintain a public facade that it remained intact and invincible.

By the time World War I had come to an end, IWW leaders had jettisoned the bravado. The union was in disarray, its membership having drastically declined, and dozens of its leaders were confronting long prison sentences. In evaluating the post-war situation, Haywood abandoned his earlier posture to present a more sober and realistic analysis. Unfortunately, by 1919 it was too late.

Two years earlier, in the summer of 1917, the IWW had reached the peak of its strength. Its membership soared as it conducted successful strikes in key industries. Of course, this success drew the hostile attention of the federal government. There was no easy answer to the harsh repressive measures directed at the IWW, but more should have been done to ensure the union's survival as an effective organization.

Haywood held a position of influence. He therefore bears a significant share of the responsibility for the failure of the IWW to adequately cope with the wave of repression he so eloquently describes in the following letter circulated as a fundraiser for the union's General Defense Committee.

DOCUMENT SEVEN[5]

Circular Letter

William Haywood

[1919]

BREAK THE CONSPIRACY

When I was leaving the Leavenworth penitentiary, under bond of $15,000, having served eleven months of a twenty-year sentence, with a $20,000 fine hanging over me, a fellow convict, not a fellow worker, said to me, "Put on the soft pedal, Bill." My reply was that the soft pedal never got a man into the penitentiary, and, likewise, it would never get a man out. My efforts on the outside would be to liberate my fellow workers from this and other prisons.

To open the jail doors I knew it would require publicity, and much of it, of a different kind than the people have ever read or heard of before. Sentiments must be changed. The truth must be told. The workers must be made to understand that the imprisoned members of the Industrial Workers of the World were the victims of the blackest and most vicious conspiracy ever conceived in the minds of men.

It was the purpose of the employing class, the so-called business element, to crush the I.W.W., to tear it out by the roots. To do this they used, and are still using, their political henchmen and the overwhelming power of the venal press.

For many years past, the I.W.W. has been under the constant surveillance of that branch of government termed the Department of Justice. The never-closing eyes of many detective agencies have been continually upon us. Police departments have been ever alert watching the I.W.W. for infractions of the law.

The mystic, magic letters, I.W.W., have, by the newspapers, been associated with all manner of heinous crimes, charging us with things that the membership of the organization never dreamed of—much less committed.

These fearful things were harped upon by august senators of the upper house; an erstwhile governor, the elongated, bald-headed Thomas of Colorado, ranted and fumed about the I.W.W. conniving and thriving on German gold.[6] Unconsciously, perhaps, the senator of the Centennial state became a party to the base conspiracy, but his prattling and infantile assertions were refuted by government witnesses upon the stand as bank experts and accountants testified that the books of the I.W.W. were kept in excellent shape, and not a trace of German gold was to be found.

Miserable stories were circulated about the poisoning of blooded breeds of cattle, or putting ground glass in foodstuffs. Such fearful crimes, if perpetrated, could have only been the acts of the insane, but were written by vicious brain reporters and published by the daily papers, either charged directly to, or in some way connected with, the I.W.W. Nothing was too vile or reprehensible for these white-livered pencil pushers to charge against the I.W.W. There was no way to refute their infamous villainous lies that they so malignantly told about us. The daily press, then as now, was closed to the truth.

Treacherous labor fakers, like Gompers and his ilk, countenanced the brutal assaults and pernicious persecution upon the membership of the I.W.W., not because they thought we were guilty of the offenses as charged, but because, forsooth, they regard the I.W.W. as a rival organization. These A.F. Of L. officials are contemptible tools of the employing class. They have now shown their polluted hands to the general membership, and their traitorous official days with labor unions are numbered.

It was in such an atmosphere, generated by slanderous tongue, malicious story-telling, lying politicians, at a time when the war fever had overheated the blood of the nation, when the people were not in a normal state of mind, that hundreds of members of the I.W.W. were forced to trial. The inevitable result was conviction; as one of the jurors said to our counsel, "If your names had been on the list, you would have gone to the Leavenworth penitentiary with the rest." It was to this federal penitentiary that we of the Chicago group of the I.W.W. came to serve long terms of imprisonment. Ninety-three of us, mostly young, strong men, and not a criminal among the number.

Later came the Sacramento trial. The men who stood before the bar of justice in the Capitol city of the Golden state decided that any kind of defense was worse than useless, so they adopted the resolution of "Silence." No man uttered a word during the progress of this remarkable trial. All of the "Silent Defenders" were convicted, and they too were sent to the Leavenworth penitentiary.[7]

During these strenuous days, many hundreds of members of the I.W.W. were jailed, arrested without warrant, and held without charge. Thousands were drafted, more were held for investigation and deportation, while others were driven from pillar to post. Free America had become surcharged with the virulent spirit of blackest Russia under the regime of Czar Nicholas, before the coming of the revolution now offering cheer and comfort to the workers of the world.

There is no gainsaying the fact that the I.W.W. was crippled. The Department of Justice shook the organization as a bulldog shakes an empty sack.

We are appealing the Chicago and Sacramento cases. The financial cost will be tremendous, but we are determined to give normal and rational minded judges an opportunity to review the meager evidence against us. We urge you to be alert and open-minded. The decisions in these cases are of as much importance to you as to the men in prison, or to those of us who will have to go back to prison if these cases are not reversed.

Watch the trials of the I.W.W. in Michigan, Nebraska, California,

Washington and Oregon, which are now on, and the Kansas trial of the forty-two men which begins at Kansas City, Kansas, December 1, 1919. These men have been confined for over two years in some of the vilest jails of the country. The Sedgwick county jail, a revolving contraption, has recently been condemned. Here these men were held while indictments were framed and quashed, until now, after two years' imprisonment, they are to go to trial under the third indictment.[8] "Their only crime is loyalty to the working class." Will you be loyal to yourself and them? It is all they ask. All that any of us ask is a square deal. This we are going to have from now on. Our backs are against the wall. This conspiracy against the Industrial Workers of the World, and the working class generally, must be broken. We do not ask you to help if it hurts you, but assure you it will hurt you worse later if you don't help now.

  Yours for Industrial Freedom,
   William D. Haywood, Secretary

Conclusion

In spite of the draconian repression it experienced during the World War I, the Industrial Workers of the World continues to this day to be a focal point for radicals interested in workplace organizing. During the last years, the IWW has initiated organizing drives among Starbucks coffee shop workers and fast food workers in Minnesota. Furthermore, the impact of the IWW and its history goes far beyond its ranks. Joe Hill songs are still sung on picket lines and activists throughout the world have heard of the union's militant struggles.

The extensive correspondence buried in the trial transcript provides new insights into the IWW as it really was at its high point, thus making it possible to go beneath the surface mythology to get a better idea of what the Wobblies actually were. These letters show the IWW as a dynamic, democratic organization, where strategy and tactics were continually being discussed. In its heyday, the IWW sought to balance the demands for local control with the need for coordinated action throughout an industry and around the country. The union also grappled with the pressure to focus on immediate demands that might be won in the short run, instead of pressing forward with a program that went beyond the confines of the existing capitalist system and looked forward to a new society based on cooperation, equality and workers' control of the entire economy. Within this context, the demand for a six-hour day was paramount. Demands for a shorter work day continue to be of critical importance to this day.

Of course, the IWW made mistakes and had its limitations. The union failed to present a coherent opposition to World War I, at a time when its rank and file members were ready to act and were pushing the union to organize a collective response to the war and the draft. In addition, the IWW primarily organized in industries where most of the workforce were men, and, as a result, its culture suffered from a certain macho bravado that made it harder to bring women into the union and integrate them into the leadership.

Still, the union learned from its mistakes, as it developed new programs and strategies. At first, the IWW promoted sabotage as an important tactic in the class struggle. The term 'sabotage' covered a wide variety of tactics, including low-level damage of corporate property. Yet in the summer of 1917, when the union organized effective mass strikes among copper miners and lumberjacks, Wobblies went out of their way to avoid violence and confrontations. Shortly afterward, the IWW explicitly rejected the use of sabotage, a position it upholds to this day.

Imperfect as it was, the IWW remains a heroic example of working class resistance. A study of its history can still provide us with important insights. It has been more than a century since the union was founded, and the world has changed a great deal since then. The workforce in the United States and Western Europe has been drastically altered as manufacturing and mining is outsourced to the developing countries. Nevertheless, there are lessons to be learned, particularly since many of the problems confronted by the IWW are still difficult issues for radicals today. We need to be creative in making use of our history, just as the IWW militants learned from the past while creatively developing tactics and strategies to overcome the obstacles they confronted.

Suggested Readings

Most of the correspondence in this books has been drawn from the complete transcript of the Chicago IWW conspiracy trial of 1918. The transcript can be found in the records of the Army's Military Intelligence Department, Record Group 165, File 10110-120 in the National Archives in College Park, Maryland.

This is a brief list of books that look at the issues raised in this anthology. A more complete bibliography can be found in my *Wobblies in Their Heyday*.

I. Introduction and Overall Histories

Chester, Eric. *The Wobblies in Their Heyday: The Industrial Workers of the World During the World War I Era* (Amherst, MA: Levellers Press, 2016).

Dubofsky, Melvyn. *We Shall Be All: A History of the Industrial Workers of the World* (Chicago: Quadrangle Books, 1969).

II. Centralization

Hall, Covington. *Labor Struggles in the Deep South and Other Writings* (Charles H. Kerr, 1999).

III. Violence

Adler, William, M. *The Man Who Never Died: The Life, Times and Legacy of Joe Hill* (New York, Bloomsbury, 2011).

McGuckin, Henry. *Memoirs of a Wobbly* (Chicago, Charles H. Kerr).

Rosemont, Franklin. *Joe Hill: The IWW and the Making of a Revolutionary Working Class Culture* (Chicago: Charles H. Kerr, 2002)

IV. Sabotage

Foner, Philip Sheldon. *History of the Labor Movement in the United States, Volume 4: The Industrial Workers of the World, 1905-1917*.

Hall, Greg. *Harvest Wobblies: The Industrial Workers of the World and Agricultural Laborers in the American West, 1905-1930* (Corvallis: Oregon State University, 2001).

V. Opposing the War and VI. Conscription

Chester, *Wobblies in Their Heyday*
Dubofsky, *We Shall Be All*

VII Repression

Gambs, John S., *The Decline of the IWW* (New York, Columbia University Press, 1932).

Preston, William. *Aliens and Dissenters: Federal Suppression of Radicals, 1903-1933* (Cambridge, Mass.: Harvard University Press, 1963).

VIII. Bisbee

Byrkit, James W. *Forging the Copper Collar: Arizona's Management War of 1901-1921* (Tucson: University of Arizona Press, 1982).

Jensen, Vernon. *Heritage of Conflict: Labor Relations in the Nonferrous Metals Industry up to 1930* (Ithaca: N.Y.: Cornell University Press, 1950).

IX. Lumberjacks

Hyman, Harold Melvin. *Soldiers and Spruce: Origins of the Loyal Legion of Loggers and Lumbermen* (Los Angeles: Institute of Industrial Relations, University of California, 1963).

Tyler, Robert L. *Rebels of the Woods: The IWW in the Pacific Northwest* (Eugene: University of Oregon, 1967).

X. Frank Little

Byrnes, Mike and Lee Rickey, *The Truth About the Lynching of Frank Little* (Butte: Old Butte Publishing, 2003).

Calvert, Jerry W. *Gibraltar: Socialism and Labor in Butte, Montana, 1895-1920* (Helena: Montana Historical Society, 1988).

Chronology

June 27 to July 8, 1905: The founding convention of the Industrial Workers of the World is held in Chicago, Illinois.

December 30, 1905: Former governor of Idaho, Frank Steunenberg, is assassinated by a bomb. Leaders of the Western Federation of Miners, William Haywood, Charles Moyer and Pettibone are arrested for the killing. After lengthy trials, Haywood and Moyer are acquitted.

December 21, 1911: Big Bill Haywood addresses a large audience at Cooper Union in New York City, and defends the McNamara brothers and the use of sabotage. His speech triggers an intense debate within the Socialist Party.

December 1, 1912: Anaconda institutes rustling card system. This establishes a tight system of screening each job applicant, allowing Anaconda to weed out those it views as undesirables.

February 1913: Haywood is recalled from the National Executive Committee of the Socialist Party. He responds by resigning from the Party, and he is joined by thousands of members of its left-wing.

August 3, 1913: At a mass rally held in support of a strike of agricultural workers, shooting breaks out between strikers and sheriff's deputies. Four are killed, including the district attorney. Soon after, Richard (Blackie) Ford and Herman Suhr are charged with murder.

January 10, 1914: Two armed men enter a grocery store in Salt Lake City, and the resulting shooting leads to the death of two men. Joe Hill is arrested and charged with murder three days later.

January 31, 1914: Ford and Suhr are convicted of 2nd degree murder of District Attorney Edmund Manwell. Six days later, the two are sentenced to life imprisonment by Judge Eugene McDaniel.

June 28, 1914: Joe Hill convicted of murder and sentenced to death after a lengthy trial.

April 15, 1915: The Agricultural Workers' Organization is formed at a convention held in Kansas City, Missouri. The union grows rapidly and becomes the largest affiliate of the IWW.

Summer and Autumn 1915: The IWW initiates a systematic effort to free Ford and Suhr by threatening to burn California's agricultural crops.

September 8, 1915: James Schmidt, a migrant worker who had been riding for free on a freight train, becomes involved in a shootout in Aberdeen, South Dakota with Ross Farrar, a railroad brakeman. Schmidt is accused of murder and the IWW organizes for his defense. The jury fails to reach a verdict and Schmidt is freed.

September 11, 1915: Governor Johnson rejects any commutation of the prison sentences of Ford and Suhr, insisting he will not be intimidated by IWW threats.

November 19, 1915: Joe Hill executed by firing squad.

December 1915: Delegates to a statewide conference of the California section of the Agricultural Workers' Organization, an IWW affiliate, do not discuss the campaign to free Ford and Suhr, but concentrate instead on organizing migrant workers in the fields. Threats of arson rapidly diminish afterward.

February 1916: Metal Mine Workers' Industrial Union #490 chartered by the General Executive Board of the Industrial Workers of the World with jurisdiction over the iron ore miners in northern Minnesota.

November 20 to December 1, 1916: Tenth convention of the IWW held in Chicago. Delegates vote to fund organizing drive in copper fields of Arizona. Publication of *Solidarity*, the union's newspaper, is shifted to Chicago headquarters. Affiliated unions limited to one industry. Shortly afterward, Agricultural Workers' Organization is renamed the Agricultural Workers' Industrial Union #400.

January 1917: General Executive Board charters the Metal Mine Workers' Industrial Union #800 with jurisdiction over Western states hardrock miners. Grover Perry opens Phoenix headquarters and begins dispatching organizers to copper camps throughout Arizona. Frank Little and Grover Perry lead this organizing effort.

March 3-5, 1917: Lumber Workers' Industrial Union #500 founded at convention held in Spokane, Washington. Delegates call for strike in support of eight-hour day. Soon afterward, strikes begin at lumber camps in Idaho and spread throughout the Pacific Northwest. Delegates also urge the IWW to resist conscription.

April 6, 1917: Congress declares war on Germany. The United States enters World War I.

May 18, 1917: Congress passes Selective Service Act. This statute establishes a procedure to be used to conscript men into the military that has been followed in every war since then, when needed.

June 1, 1917: The North Dakota Nonpartisan League votes to open negotiations with the Agricultural Workers' Industrial Union on an agreement covering migrant farm workers in that state. The contract is quickly negotiated and the AWIU leadership tentatively accepts it, but the NPL leadership rejects the contract since the wage increases it incorporates are viewed as too generous.

June 5, 1917: All young men between the ages of twenty-one and thirty-nine are required to register for the draft. IWW and radical Irish nationalists organize a mass protest in Butte on the eve of registration day. The peaceful march is dispersed by local police and federal troops using bayonets.

June 8, 1917: A fire breaks out in the Granite Mountain mine in Butte and quickly spreads to a twin shaft, the Speculator. One hundred and sixty-eight miners are killed, the worst accident in the history of hardrock mining in the United States. Soon after, a spontaneous strike shuts down Butte's mines to protest the dangerous violations of safety procedures.

June 13, 1917: Formation of Butte Metal Mine Workers' Union by a coalition of radicals that includes IWW members and those linked to the left-wing of the Socialist Party. The BMMWU functions as an independent union.

June 15, 1917: Congress enacts the Espionage Act with President Wilson's approval. Title 1, Section 3, gives the Justice Department far-reaching powers to prosecute anyone opposing the war or the draft.

June 17, 1917: A statewide meeting of the Metal Mine Workers' Industrial Union #800 is held in Bisbee, Arizona. Plans for a strike of copper miners are laid but a specific date is not set.

June 20, 1917: Frank Little suffers a broken bone in his ankle when a car he is in traveling from Bisbee, Arizona, to Globe, Arizona, goes over a cliff. Little has to use crutches from that point on.

June 27, 1917: Bisbee branch of the MMWIU calls strike that shuts down the area's mines. The strike quickly spreads to other mining districts in Arizona, in particular Globe and Jerome.

June 29 to July 6, 1917: The IWW's General Executive Board meets in Chicago. Frank Little urges the GEB to issue statement declaring its open opposition to the war and urging IWW members to resist the draft.

July 5, 1917: Federal troops occupy Globe to suppress the strike of miners in the district. Picket lines are dispersed and IWW meetings are disrupted.

July 11, 1917: Armed vigilantes in Jerome round up more than one hundred miners. After a screening process, sixty-seven are deported, and most never return. The deportation crushes the strike called by the IWW's Metal Mine Workers' Union #800.

July 12, 1917: Hundreds of armed vigilantes acting under authority of the local sheriff deport nearly twelve hundred miners from Bisbee. The miners are dumped in the New Mexico desert. For months after, vigilantes screen everyone entering Bisbee. The deportation ends all union organization in Bisbee.

July 12, 1917: Butte Metal Mine Workers' Union calls for the creation of new nationwide industrial union for miners and issues a call for a founding conference to be held in Denver on August 1. Haywood, acting for the IWW, accepts the plan for a new union of miners and urges IWW affiliated branches of miners to send delegates to the Denver conference.

July 17, 1917: Frank Little leaves Salt Lake City, where he has been conferring with Grover Perry, and travels to Butte. He will spend the next two weeks speaking with Butte union leaders, speaking out against the war, and urging Butte's miners to adopt more militant non-violent tactics.

July 19, 1917: Little speaks at mass rally of striking miners held at Butte ballpark. Denounces the use of federal troops to quash strikes.

July 28, 1917: Ralph Chaplin's editorial on conscription is printed in *Solidarity*. The editorial criticizes conscription but urges IWW members to register for the draft and then claim exemptions as conscientious objectors.

August 1, 1917: Frank Little is lynched by masked vigilantes who abduct him from his room in a boarding house, drag him from a vehicle, and then hang him from a railroad trestle on the outskirts of Butte. No one is ever prosecuted for this murder.

August 10, 1917: Federal troops begin to patrol the streets of Butte. Troops will occupy Butte until April 1921.

August 19, 1917: Lumber Workers' Union leaders arrested in Spokane, Washington and detained indefinitely by Army soldiers. These arrests are intended to prevent a general strike called for the next day to include the entire Pacific Northwest. The strike call fails.

September 5, 1917: Nationwide raids led by Bureau of Investigation agents ransack IWW halls across country. At the union's Chicago headquarters, government agents carry away a huge assortment of documents, which are never returned to the union.

September 28, 1917: 165 IWW leaders and activists indicted by federal grand jury in Chicago

December 17, 1917: Bomb explosion destroys stairs of governor's mansion in Sacramento, California. Dozens of IWW members arrested during the next two weeks. They are held on high bail in appalling conditions.

April 1, 1918: Trial of 113 IWW leaders and activists begins in the Chicago district federal court. Judge Kenesaw Mountain Landis presides.

May 21, 1918: Sedition Act becomes law when signed by President Wilson after approval of Congress. The statute amends the Espionage Act to make it even more repressive.

August 17, 1918: Jury deliberates for 55 minutes and then convicts 100 IWW members on four counts of violating the Espionage Act at the conclusion of the Chicago trial that has lasted more than four months.

August 30, 1918: Judge Landis imposes lengthy sentences on 93 of those convicted to be served at Leavenworth Federal Penitentiary, a maximum security prison. Many defendants are sentenced to terms of ten and twenty years for violating the Espionage Act.

January 16, 1919: In Sacramento, Judge Frank Rudkin sentences forty-three IWW members to lengthy terms in jail after a jury finds them guilty of violating the Espionage Act and carrying out acts of sabotage. Many of those convicted receive ten-year prison sentences.

April 21, 1920: Shooting on the Anaconda Road in Butte. One killed and fifteen wounded. Three days later, Anaconda Mining discharges all IWW members. Efforts to organize Butte's copper miners finally been crushed.

October 5, 1920: U.S. 7th Circuit Court reverses the convictions of the Chicago trial on two counts, but affirms the jury's guilty verdict on the charge of violating the Espionage Act by obstructing the draft. The IWW prisoners must therefore serve the lengthy prison sentences imposed by Judge Landis.

March 31, 1921: Haywood flees the United States and reappears in the Soviet Union. He thereby forfeits a bond of $15,000.

April 11, 1921: U.S. Supreme Court refuses to hear the appeal of the Chicago IWW case. Shortly afterward, eight IWW leaders who are out on bail disappear and forfeit their bonds. The IWW suffers a huge financial loss.

June 21, 1923: President Harding offers to commute the sentences of many of the IWW members at Leavenworth if they agree to abide by the law when released. Most accept the terms and are released, but those who refuse condemn the prisoners who are freed.

December 15, 1923: President Calvin Coolidge unconditionally pardons the remainder of the IWW prisoners.

October 1924: The IWW convention splits with one group forming a new organization, the Emergency Program. A major factor in the split stems from the bitter disagreements that arose among the IWW prisoners in Leavenworth in responding to the government's amnesty proposals.

Glossary

Individuals

Brazier, Richard (1882-): Born in England. Came to Canada in 1903 and moved to U.S. in 1906. Worked as a migrant farm worker and miner. Joined the IWW in 1908. Lived in Spokane, Washington from 1909. Secretary of the IWW joint council in Spokane in 1911. Elected to General Executive Board in 1914. A defendant in the Chicago conspiracy trial and received twenty year sentence. Released from Leavenworth Federal Penitentiary in 1923. Worked on a tugboat in New York City harbor. Remained active in radical politics up through the 1960s.

Chaplin, Ralph Hosea (1887-1961): Born in Kansas, but moved as a child to Chicago. Worked as a graphic designer. Joined the Socialist Party soon after its formation in 1901. Active in support of coal miners' strike in West Virginia in 1912-13. Joined the IWW soon afterward. Wrote several popular songs, including "Solidarity Forever," and drew cartoons for Wobbly papers. Edited *Solidarity* from the early spring of 1917 to his arrest in September 1917. Sentenced to twenty years at Chicago trial. Released from Leavenworth in June 1923. Remained active in the IWW, and editor of *Industrial Worker* from 1932 to 1936. A staunch anti-Communist, and critic of the New Deal, he left the IWW in 1936. Moved to Tacoma, Washington in 1941 and edited the local AFL newspaper.

Haywood, William Dudley (1869-1928): Went to work at age fifteen as a miner. In 1894, joined the Western Federation of Miners. Elected its secretary-treasurer in 1900. Chaired the founding convention of the Industrial Workers of the World in June 1905. Arrested for killing the former governor of Idaho, Frank Steunenberg, in February 1906, but acquitted in July 1907. From 1908 to 1912, he traveled around the country speaking for the Socialist Party. Elected to the Party's National Executive Committee in 1912, but recalled from office in February

1913 in a dispute over the use of sabotage. Elected general secretary-treasurer of the Industrial Workers of the World in November 1914. Indicted in September 1917 for violating the Espionage Act, convicted and sentenced to a twenty-year term in August 1918. Jumped bail in March 1921 and went to the Soviet Union. Soon became disillusioned, but remained there until his death.

Lambert, Charles L. (1881?-1961?): Born in Scotland and immigrated to the United States in 1905. Worked as an unskilled laborer in oil fields and on construction sites. Joined IWW in 1911. Secretary of the Ford and Suhr Defense Committee in 1914-1915. Elected to the IWW's General Executive Board in 1916. Indicted on conspiracy charges in September 1917 and sentenced to twenty years in prison. Agreed to deportation back to Britain in 1922. Became a diamond prospector in British Guiana and then worked for a London bookmaker.

Little, Frank H. (1877?-1917): Raised in Oklahoma. Started working as a miner in 1900, and became active in the Western Federation of Miners. Organizer for the IWW beginning in 1906. Arrested during the free speech fights in Fresno, California and Missoula, Missouri. Elected to the IWW's General Executive Board in 1914. Badly beaten by vigilantes in 1916 while organizing iron miners in the Mesabi Range of Minnesota. In January 1917, he was sent to organize Arizona's copper miners. Sent to Butte, Montana in July 1917 to help miners' strike. Openly opposed U.S. participation in World War I. Lynched in Butte on August 1, 1917.

Moyer, Charles H. (1866-1929): Born in Iowa. Worked as a silver miner in Black Hills of South Dakota. Became president of the Deadwood local of the Western Federation of Miners in 1894. Elected to the executive board of the Western Federation of Miners in 1899 and became its president in 1902. Supported the formation of the IWW in 1905. Arrested in February 1906 for assassination of former governor Frank Steunenberg. Held without bail for nearly two years. Released without trial in January 1908. Rejected radical politics and led the WFM into the American Federation of Labor in 1911. Remained president of union until forced out in 1926. Lived quietly in California in retirement.

Nef, Walter T. (1882-): Born in Switzerland. Came to the U.S. in 1901. Worked as a lumberjack in Pacific Northwest. Joined the IWW in 1908. Elected secretary of the Agricultural Workers' Organization at its founding conference in March 1915. Created delegate system to collect dues. Quit AWO in November 1916 after dispute with Haywood. Became secretary of the IWW's Maritime Workers' Union in Philadelphia. Avoided any opposition to the war effort. One of the defendants at the Chicago conspiracy trial and received twenty year sentence. Released from Leavenworth Federal Penitentiary in 1922.

Rowan, James (1878-?): Born in Ireland. Came to the U.S. in 1897. Worked as a granite cutter in New England. Moved to Pacific Northwest in 1911 and worked as a lumberjack. Joined the IWW in 1912. Elected the secretary of the Lumber Workers' Union #500 at its founding conference in March 1917. Interned by the military in August 1917 and detained for a month before being transferred to Chicago as a defendant in the conspiracy trial. Sentenced to twenty years in jail. One of the last IWW prisoners to be released in December 1923. Instrumental in 1924 split within the IWW. Formed the Emergency Program which ceased to exist in 1930.

St. John, Vincent (1876-1929): Born in Kentucky. Became a coal miner at seventeen. Became president of Telluride Miners' Union in 1900 and led bitter strike there a year later. Active in the IWW from its formation in 1905. Shot in hand during Goldfield, Nevada strike in 1906. Suffered from bronchitis from mining and eventually died from its complications. General Secretary-Treasurer of IWW from 1908 to 1914. In early 1915 left union and began prospecting for gold in New Mexico. One of the defendants in Chicago trial and received ten year sentence. Released from Leavenworth in 1922 and went back to prospecting, but died in poverty in San Francisco.

Sheridan, Don (1884-?): Born in Scotland. Moved to the United States in 1907. In Washington, worked as a migrant farm laborer and a lumberjack. Joined the IWW in 1912 and became the secretary of the Spokane local in 1914. Interim secretary of the Lumber Workers' Union #500 in the spring of 1917. In September 1917, was indicted in the Chicago conspiracy trial and sentenced to ten years in jail. Released from Leavenworth Penitentiary in August 1923.

Organizations

Bureau of Investigation: Formed in June 1908 to serve as the intelligence agency for the Department of Justice collecting information on antitrust cases. A small agency until April 1917, when the United States declared war on Germany. The Bureau of Investigation was given the primary responsibility for investigating cases arising out of the Espionage Act and other statutes aimed at anti-war dissidents. Grew rapidly during war, opening field offices around the country. Worked closely with the War Emergency Division. Bruce Bielaski served as its chief during this period. Renamed the Federal Bureau of Investigation in July 1935.

Industrial Workers of the World: Founded in June 1905 at a Chicago convention. Initiated by the Western Federation of Miners, although the two unions soon became bitter enemies. Committed to militant direct action and the end of the capitalist market economy. Involved in several free speech fights from 1909 to 1913. During World War I, successfully organized migrant agricultural workers, lumberjacks and copper miners. Became the primary target of federal repression. In August 1918, ninety-three leading members of the IWW were convicted of violating the Espionage Act and sentenced to long terms in prison. Pressures exerted by the unrelenting repression at state and federal levels led to demoralization and splits. Survived as a much smaller union.

Western Federation of Miners: Formed in 1893 out of a merger of several local unions. Engaged in several bitter strikes during the following years. Withdrew from the American Federation of Labor in 1897. Adopted a socialist program in 1901. Sponsored the formation of the Industrial Workers of the World in 1905, but withdrew two years later. Rejoined the American Federation of Labor in 1911. Renamed the International Mine, Mill and Smelter Workers in 1916. Joined the CIO in 1935, but expelled for Communist influence in 1950. Merged into the United Steel Workers' Union in 1967

Notes

Chapter One: Introduction

1 Melvyn Dubofsky, *We Shall Be All: A History of the Industrial Workers of the World* (Chicago: Quadrangle Books, 1969), p. 332.

Chapter Two: The Centralization Issue

1 Paul Brissenden, *The IWW: A Study of American Syndicalism* (New York: Columbia University Press, 1919), p. 326; Melvyn Dubofsky, We Shall Be All: A History of the Industrial Workers of the World (Chicago: Quadrangle Books, 1969), p. 243.

2 Robert Tyler, *Rebels of the Woods: The IWW in the Pacific Northwest* (Eugene: University of Oregon Press, 1967), pp. 88-9.

3 At the September 1914 convention, the decentralizers succeeded in passing a constitutional amendment permitting a membership referendum to determine policy when ten locals were prepared to endorse the proposal. Brissenden, *IWW*, p. 334.

4 Part of the dues paid by each IWW member was earmarked and sent to the Chicago headquarters to maintain the central office and employ a staff of national organizers. Indeed, Thompson was being paid out of these funds. Thus, St. John is proposing an arrangement, presumably one for a specified, short period of time, under which these funds would be returned to the newly affiliated union in the lumber industry. Such an arrangement would have had to have the approval of the General Executive Board before being implemented.

5 C.J. Folsom had been the president of the Shingle Weavers' Union, but by 1913 he was working as a staff organizer for the Washington State American Federation of Labor. In this capacity, he wrote an article condemning the IWW, and urging the Shingle Weavers' Union to reject the effort to leave the AFL and join the IWW.

6 Bill Haywood had been active in the left-wing Socialist Party of America, but, after his recall from the Party's National Executive Committee in 1913, he resumed his activity in the IWW. St. John is informing Thompson that Haywood would soon join the IWW staff as General Organizer. St. John soon left the union, and Haywood was elected to replace him as General Secretary-Treasurer at the IWW's 1914 national convention.

7 St. John kept accurate statistics on the IWW's membership while he held

the post of General Secretary-Treasurer and he made those figures public. His estimate for IWW membership in 1914 is accurate.

8 Covington Hall was a journalist who had been working with an interracial union of lumberjacks in Louisiana that had affiliated with the IWW. The Louisiana union was crushed after a violent confrontation in May 1913, and Hall then moved to Portland, Oregon. He was a leading proponent of the decentralization proposal.

The *Industrial Worker* was the union's newspaper aimed at its members and supporters in the Pacific Northwest. It had been printed in Spokane, Washington from 1909 to 1913. Contrary to St. John's fears, it was not revived in Portland during the decentralization debate, although a second series was published from Seattle starting in 1916.

9 Wheat was first harvested and placed in large stacks. Threshing involved throwing the stacked wheat into a threshing machine that stripped the wheat of its husks and retained the essential grain. When one field was finished, the machinery had to be moved and set up before threshing could remove. In large farms, this might require a considerable down time.

10 This is weak, nebulous wording. It should be compared with the comparable wording in the demands submitted by the lumberjacks during their strike. Both migrant agricultural workers and lumberjacks were subject to the vagaries of temporary housing provided by employers.

Chapter Three: Sabotage

1 A muzhik was a Russian peasant in the era of the Czar. Until 1861, Russian peasants were bound to the land as serfs. After this, they were no longer formally tied to a landowner's estate, but most of them remained destitute and dependent on the local aristocracy.

2 On May 1, 1886, the Knights of Labor organized nationwide protests demanding the eight hour day. In Chicago, a large peaceful rally was held without incident. Two days later, police dispersed a picket line at the McCormick tractor works using clubs and bullets. On the following day, a group of radicals, anarchists, and left-wing socialists, organized a protest rally at Haymarket Square in the downtown district. When police on horseback charged the crowd, someone threw a bomb, killing seven police officers. The police opened fired indiscriminately, killing at least five demonstrators and wounding dozens of protestors and several police officers.

A Chicago grand jury indicted ten prominent Chicago radicals, including the organizers of the rally. The evidence linking the defendants to the bombing was minimal and, indeed, scholars have concluded that a small group of anarchists, acting independently of most of the organizers of the rally, was probably responsible for the bomb. Eight of the ten charged were convicted of murder, four were hanged and one committed suicide while in jail. The rest of the Haymarket defendants were pardoned by Governor John Peter Altgeld in June 1893.

3 The four men mentioned in the editorial were those who were hanged after having been convicted of conspiracy to commit murder following the Haymarket incident. A fifth person, Louis Lingg, committed suicide prior to his planned execution.

4 William Haywood, Charles Moyer, and George Pettibone were charged with conspiracy to murder former Idaho governor Frank Steunenberg on December 30, 1905. The prosecution's case rested on the testimony of Harry Orchard, who claimed that he had undertaken numerous acts of violence, including the assassination of Steunenberg, on orders from the three defendants as leaders of the Western Federation of Miners. The three were held without bail for a year in an Idaho jail. Haywood was tried first and defended by Clarence Darrow in one of the most dramatic trials in U.S. history. After his acquittal in July 1907, Pettibone was tried and acquitted. Moyer was then released without being tried.

To this day, the question of who killed Steunenberg and why remains unresolved and fiercely debated.

5 Joseph Ettor, the IWW's General Organizer, and Arturo Giovannitti, the secretary of the Italian federation of the Socialist Party, were sent by the IWW to organize the 1912 strike of textile workers in Lawrence, Massachusetts. They were charged with the murder of Anna LoPizzo, a striker shot while picketing by a police officer, although neither of the two IWW organizers was anywhere near the site of the shooting. After a lengthy trial, they were acquitted in November 1912.

6 A few words are missing from the microfilm versions of this editorial, so I have inserted appropriate words to fill in the gaps.

7 *Solidarity*, March 6, 1915.

8 The pardon hearing was held before Governor Johnson on March 5, 1915. Representatives of the California Federation of Labor spoke in favor of the pardon request.

9 Maxwell McNutt was a prominent progressive attorney in the San Francisco Bay Area. He later served as an attorney for Tom Mooney and went on to become a judge.

10 George Speed was the secretary of the San Francisco IWW. A veteran activist who had been involved in radical politics well before the founding of the IWW, he was considerably older than most of the union's militants.

11 *Solidarity*, September 18, 1915. This is a reprint of an article dated September 1, 1915, and circulated by the International News Service, the news agency for the Hearst newspapers.

12 The Commission on Industrial Relations was created by Congress in 1912 to examine labor relations throughout the United States and to deliver a report with recommendations for changes in the government's policy and legislation in this area of concern. Woodrow Wilson appointed the members of the commission, including its chair, Frank P. Walsh, who, although generally sympathetic to unions, was definitely hostile to the radical politics of the IWW. The Commission heard testimony from 1912 to 1915 from a range of corporate executives, union officials and rank and file members, before issuing a report in 1916 in eleven volumes. Haywood testified before the Commission, and presented the IWW's perspective on the need for radical change through industrial action. Other IWW leaders testified before the Commission as well.

13 The California Commission of Immigration and Housing was the state agency that coordinated California's efforts to suppress the IWW. It had no secretary in August 1915, but Lambert probably met with Paul Scharrenberg, the secretary of the California Federation of Labor and a member of the Commission of Immigration and Housing.

14 On August 13, 1915, the Sacramento Bee printed an article that the "inner circle" of the IWW was planning a campaign of arson against California's agricultural industry. Already there had been a major fire of unknown origin in a cannery in San Jose on August 7, 1915. The California Commission of Immigration and Housing issued a confidential warning to the industry and cannery owners were taking precautions to discharge all employees who were viewed as "suspicious characters."

15 On September 11, 1915, Governor Johnson issued a statement denying any reduction in the sentences being served by Ford and Suhr, insisting he would not consider clemency as long as the IWW threatened violence and sabotage.

16 Criminal syndicalism laws made it illegal to advocate the use of violence or sabotage to bring about social or economic change. These laws went further in making it illegal to be a member of any organization that advocated such actions. These laws were aimed at the IWW and courts ruled that the prosecution did not need to prove that the defendant had done or said anything. Membership in the IWW combined with possession of union literature, or even a Wobbly song book, was sufficient to demonstrate an active participation in a criminal conspiracy.

Criminal syndicalism legislation was first enacted in Idaho in March 1917, but quickly spread throughout the West. In most states, the legislation was used as a threat, and as a means of rounding up and detaining troublemakers, although only a few IWW leaders were actually tried under its provisions and sentenced to lengthy prison terms. In California in the period from 1918 to 1925, hundreds of IWW members were jailed under the criminal syndicalism statute in a concerted effort to eliminate the union from that state.

17 Harvey Duff, *The Silent Defenders, Courts and Capitalism in California* (Chicago: IWW, [1920], pp. 101-02.

18 "Resolution Regarding Sabotage," *One Big Union Monthly* (April 1920) 1:56.

Chapter Four: Violence

1 In late 1913, coal miners shut down mines throughout Colorado, as the United Mine Workers' Union, an AFL affiliate, went on strike to win recognition, higher wages and the enforcement of mine safety laws. The mining corporations retaliated by hiring strikebreakers and forcibly moving the strikers from their company owned houses. Tent camps were established near the mines, with hundreds of miners and their families in each. Militants foraged from these camps in efforts to keep strikebreakers from the mines. On April 20, 1914, corporate gunmen employed by the Colorado Fuel and Iron Company, which was owned by John D. Rockefeller, attacked one of these tent camps near Ludlow, Colorado. After a day-long gun battle, with several fatalities resulting, the gunmen burned down the site. Eleven children and two women who had hidden in a hole beneath one of the tents died in the fire. The incident caused a huge furore. Woodrow Wilson responded by dispatching federal troops, and the violence subsided. Nevertheless, the strike was broken. John D. Rockefeller Jr. then fostered the creation of company unions as an alternative to the United Mine Workers.

2 Elizabeth Gurley Flynn was the most prominent woman in the IWW and one of its national organizers. Flynn and Hill exchanged several letters while he was in prison. As a result, Hill became convinced that the union should do more to bring women into the organization. He wrote this article for Solidarity and he also wrote the song Rebel Girl, both as a tribute to Flynn and as an encouragement to women interested in the IWW. Flynn and Hill met for the sole time in the Salt Lake City, Utah, prison in the weeks prior to his execution.

3 William Spry, a conservative Republican, served as governor of Utah from 1908 to 1916. He resisted every effort to persuade him to grant Hill executive clemency. Spry received death threats after Hill's execution, but he died a natural death in 1929.

4 Brazier was one of the IWW leaders indicted by a Chicago grand jury in September 1917. He was convicted of violating the Espionage Act and sentenced to twenty years in prison. After his release from Leavenworth in 1923, he moved to New York, where he worked on a tugboat and as a door man in an apartment building. He remained active in radical politics into 1960s, while writing on the IWW in its heyday.

5 Haywood was indicted in September 1917 for violating the Espionage

Act, and convicted and sentenced to a twenty-year term in August 1918. He jumped bail in March 1921 and went to the Soviet Union. Although he soon became disillusioned, Haywood remained there until his death in 1924.

6 Joe Hill was executed on November 19, 1915, the day Brazier wrote this letter to Haywood.

7 Passages in the Old Testament do prescribe "an eye for an eye" as a basis for a just punishment system. The Mosaic code refers to the rules set forth in the Old Testament.

8 Haywood was arranging for IWW branches around the country to hold memorial services for Joe Hill. Since Hill had asked that his body not be buried in Utah, he was cremated and his ashes were distributed to branches in key cities.

9 A "yegg" was slang for a safe-cracker or a burglar.

10 The Chicago and Northwestern was one of the most important railroad lines traversing the Dakotas and the Upper Midwest.

11 These were considerable sums in 1915. One thousand dollars, the retainer the attorney was requesting, would be the equivalent of more than $20,000 in current dollars. The willingness of the IWW to pay such a fee is indicative of how important the case seemed to the union.

Chapter Five: The Bisbee Copper Strike of 1917

1 Delegates to the July 1916 convention changed the name of the union from the Western Federation of Miners to the International Union of Mine, Mill and Smelter Workers. To avoid confusion, I refer throughout to the union as the Western Federation of Miners.

2 Perry was one of the IWW leaders indicted by the Chicago grand jury in September 1917 for violating the Espionage Act. He was convicted and sentenced to serve ten years in a federal penitentiary. Out on bail, Perry disappeared in April 1921, when the U.S. Supreme Court refused to hear the appeal of the Chicago conspiracy trial. He never emerged from hiding.

3 Charles Moyer served as president of the Western Federation of Miners from 1902 to 1926. Initially a socialist and a supporter of the IWW, he became increasingly conservative once entrenched in office. By 1917, Moyer had become an ardent supporter of the war effort, and a close ally of Samuel Gompers, the president of the American Federation of Labor. Moyer detested the IWW, and, at times, he was willing to act in collusion with employers to break IWW organizing drives.

4 In 1915 and 1916, a broad coalition of activists attempted to reform the WFM by modifying its internal structure to provide its Arizona locals with considerable autonomy. Moyer succeeded in blocking this move. The failure

of this effort created the basis for the IWW's successful organizing drive beginning in January 1917.

5 Piecard was a derogatory term used by the IWW to refer to officials within the mainstream AFL unions. The IWW frequently attacked them as overpaid and aloof from the rank and file.

6 Mining companies had recently introduced new machinery that greatly increased the amount of ore that could be stripped from the walls of the tunnels being worked for ore. These machines were very heavy, and had to be moved periodically. The companies insisted that only one miner was needed to operate these machines. The miners' struggle to require that two men operate these machines became an important demand in Arizona and elsewhere.

7 Mr. Block was a cartoon drawn by Ernest Riebe that first appeared in the Industrial Worker in 1912. Mr. Block, a cartoon figure with a square head, represented those workers who believed in the existing system and rejected the radical critique of capitalism presented by the IWW. Joe Hill wrote a song that based on the cartoon that was frequently sung by Wobblies.

8 Report, Claude McCaleb, September 26, 1917, "Synopsis of Facts," File OG 13332A, Microfilm, Records of the Bureau of Investigation, 1908-1924, Record Group 65, National Archives, College Park, Maryland.

9 There were three large mining complexes in Bisbee, as well as many smaller ones. The IWW focused its efforts on shutting down the three large mines. The Copper Queen mine was owned by Phelps Dodge, which generally set company policy for the town. Although the Calumet and Arizona mines were nearly as productive as the Copper Queen, its owners followed the lead set by Phelps Dodge. The Shattuck was the smallest of the three large mines, and it was owned by Lemuel Shattuck. Both the Copper Queen and the Calumet and Arizona brought in strikebreakers during the strike, and continued to produce copper, albeit at far lower levels than before, but the Shattuck mine shut down entirely during the strike.

10 Bill Cleary was an attorney who came to Bisbee to work for the copper companies, but soon became disillusioned and began defending injured miners suing the companies. A liberal who was active in Democratic Party politics, Cleary definitely did not share the IWW's radical critique of capitalism. Nevertheless, he supported the strike, and spoke at union rallies. Cleary was deported on July 12, 1917, and never returned to Bisbee. He moved to California and served as one of the IWW's attorneys during the 1918 trial of IWW leaders.

11 A.D. Kimball was one of the leaders of the Bisbee strike. He was indicted with more than one hundred other IWW leaders in September 1917. While incarcerated in Chicago's Cook County Jail, he became severely ill with tuberculosis. Kimball died shortly after being released from prison.

12 Gerald Sherman was superintendent of the Copper Queen mine. When

the miners heard that he had ripped up the union's demands, they were incensed.

13 Repairing the timber props that keep the roof of the excavated areas from collapsing. In other words, instead of mining ore the miners were doing maintenance work to ensure that the mine was not damaged during an extended walkout.

14 The workforce in Bisbee's copper mines was ethnically segregated. Recent immigrants from Mexico were only hired as topmen, and were excluded from jobs as miners. Topmen loaded the ore brought up from the mining shafts into railroad cars that carried the ore to smelters. The work was physically demanding and poorly paid.

The IWW gained the fervent support of Mexican workers during the 1917 strike. Its demand for a $5.50 wage rate for each shift worked represented a large jump in pay from the $3.50 per shift for topmen that prevailed prior to the strike. Indeed, the union was attempting to set the pay of topmen at a level nearly equal to that being earned by miners. Still, the IWW did not challenge the discriminatory pattern of hiring being practiced by the copper companies, although it should have done so.

15 Nippers were hired to bring new tools and tool sharpeners to miners working at the different levels of the mine. It was considered to be an entry level job, and was poorly paid. The mining companies generally employed young people to fill these positions.

16 Sheriff Harry Wheeler of Cochise County despised the IWW. From the start of the strike, he denounced the Wobblies in vitriolic terms. Wheeler directed the mass deportation of strikers on July 12, 1917. Once the strike was crushed, he joined the Army and serving in France. After the war, he returned to Arizona and lived in relative obscurity.

17 There were 4000 copper miners working in Bisbee in the summer of 1917. In addition, there were 600 topmen. The count of 5400 employees, on two shifts of 2700, would seem to include nippers, skilled workers, perhaps even foremen, in addition to miners and topmen. The IWW's support came from the miners and topmen.

18 Report, Charles E. Brennan, February 19, 1918, File OG 36190, Records of the Bureau of Investigation, Record Group 65, National Archives, College Park, Maryland.

19 The *Bisbee Review* was Bisbee's leading daily newspaper. It was owned by Phelps Dodge, which also owned the Copper Queen mine.

20 Stanley Clark, a Texan radical and an effective orator, was active in the left-wing of the Socialist Party. An attorney, and thus not a worker, he could not become a member of the union. Nevertheless, he was brought to Arizona by the IWW to speak at mass rallies. He was convicted of violating the Espionage Act in September 1917 and received a sentence of ten years. He was

released from Leavenworth Federal Penitentiary in July 1922.

21 The Bisbee Executive Committee had sent Perry a letter containing only the first paragraph of Document 3, the longer version sent to the Globe-Miami district. Clearly, Perry had also seen the more complete version, as well as the one sent to him. IWW Transcript, Government Exhibit 400, p. 8118.

22 The convention held at Bisbee in mid-June of the Metal Mine Workers' Union Industrial #800 approved the following: "We demand the six-hour day from collar to collar." The resulting thirty-six hour week would have represented a substantial decrease in the work week from the forty-eight hour week that was then the standard in the Arizona copper mines. (DEMANDS MADE BY THE FIRST CONVENTION OF METAL MINE WORKERS' INDUSTRIAL UNION 800, IWW Transcript, Government Exhibit #416, p. 9381.)

23 Perry is slightly rewording a telegram he received from Peter Kerkinen, one of the leading IWW members in Butte. The telegram sent on June 11, 1917 read: "Miners call up strike here. Thousands men. Now is the time has come when you there may start with us fight six hours day." IWW Transcript, p. 16434.

IWW members were an important segment of the Butte strike leadership, but they were in an alliance with radicals who were not IWW members. Although the Butte miners discussed the need for a six hour day, this was not one of the strike demands. The key demand concerned an end to the rustling card system whereby the Anaconda Copper Mining Company, the dominant mining company in Butte, vetted miners, and fired or refused to hire those deemed to be troublemakers.

24 When armed vigilantes approached the house of James Brew, a boilermaker at the Calumet and Arizona mine, he warned them not to approach further. When they ignored his warning, he shot and killed Orson McRae, a shift boss at the Copper Queen. Brew then put down his rifle and was shot and killed by the remaining vigilantes. No one was prosecuted for this murder.

25 Jacob Erickson, the mayor of Bisbee, was employed by Calumet and Arizona, and was closely aligned with the copper mining companies.

Chapter Six: The Lumberjack Strike of 1917

1 Alexandria, Louisiana, had been the location of conferences held by the Brotherhood of Timber Workers during its organizing efforts from 1910 until 1913. It affiliated with the IWW in 1912. Sheridan is informing Haywood that there was little possibility of a revival of this organization in the spring of 1917.

2 Eureka is a small lumber town in the northwestern corner of Montana.

3 Fortine is a logging community in northwestern Montana. St. Maries is a small town in northern Idaho.

4 The Flathead River is located in northwestern Montana, while the Stillwater River goes through southern Montana.

5 Kalispell is a town in northwestern Montana seventeen miles from Whitefish, Montana, a small logging community.

6 The Kootenai River began in Canada and then flowed through northern Idaho and northwestern Montana.

7 Libby and Troy are two small lumber towns in northwestern Montana.

8 Sabotage was frequently represented in IWW cartoons as a black cat. Presumably this was derived from popular folklore, where a black cat brought bad luck, in this case to the boss. Black cats could also travel at night without being seen, a further reason to use them as a symbol for the saboteur.

9 Sandpoint is a small lumber town in the most northern part of Idaho. The Humbird Lumber Company had built a large saw mill in Sandpoint and owned large tracts of timberland in the surrounding area.

10 A peavey is a tool used by lumberjacks to gain leverage on floating logs. It has a metal spike at one end. A sougan is a heavy woolen blanket commonly used by lumberjacks.

11 The phrase "His Master's Voice" was derived from an 1899 painting of a dog intently listening to a first-generation record player with that title. The phrase and painting were used as a trademark by one of the first makers of record players, later absorbed by RCA.

12 In this context, a bullpen is a makeshift prison, usually outdoors, used by military units to detain activists during turbulent strikes. The origins of the term are unclear, but it was already used during the 1892 strike of silver mines in the Couer d'Alene area of northern Idaho. One suggested explanation comes from the use of cattle pens for jails, with the fence surrounding the pen reinforced with barbed wire.

13 Rowan is suggesting that the timber companies tied up the Indians they had hired as strikebreakers in so much paperwork that it was easy to cheat them out of some of their earnings.

14 Bovill is a small mining town in northern Idaho. Moscow is a nearby city, also in northern Idaho.

15 The IWW frequently referred to Christian ministers, often those from the Salvation Army, as "sky pilots."

16 This is a phrase from the New Testament, the Christian Bible, but the reference is to Jesus. It reads: "the foxes have holes; the birds of the air have nests, but the Son of Man has nowhere to lay his head."

17 Sheridan was convicted at the conclusion of the Chicago conspiracy trial in August 1918. He was sentenced to ten years in jail and was only released from Leavenworth Federal Penitentiary in August 1923.

18 IWW attorneys went to the Washington Supreme Court to request that the Court order the military to provide sufficient evidence to substantiate its detention of the IWW activists. The Washington Supreme Court heard the case, but refused to issue the order. Most of the Lumber Workers' Union leaders were soon released, although Rowan remained in military detention for more than a month, when he was transferred to a Chicago prison awaiting trial with a hundred other IWW leaders from around the country charged with violating the Espionage Act. He was convicted at the conclusion of the conspiracy trial in August 1918 and given a twenty year jail sentence. Rowan was one of the last of the IWW prisoners to be released from Leavenworth Federal Penitentiary. President Calvin Coolidge commuted his sentence in December 1923.

19 The IWW affiliated Construction Workers' Industrial Union #573.

20 The IWW affiliated Railroad Workers' Industrial Union #600.

21 Criminal syndicalism laws were enacted by several Western states starting in 1917. These laws made it illegal to be a member of an organization that promoted violence or the damage of property as a means of gaining political or industrial goals. Since the IWW had advocated sabotage until the fall of 1917, membership in the union became illegal. Wobblies were sent to jail for merely being a member of the unon and possessing a song book.

22 Roy Brown was the chair of the Lumber Workers' Industrial Union. He would later become chair of the union's General Executive Board. John Turner was a key organizer in the Lumber Workers' Union. Convicted of violating the Espionage Act in the Chicago conspiracy trial, he was sentenced to ten years in prison and released from Leavenworth Federal Penitentiary in June 1923.

23 Mark Naison and Melvyn Dubofsky, eds., Microfilm, Reel 6, *Department of Justice Investigative Files, Part I: The Industrial Workers of the World* (Bethesda, Md.: University Publications of America, 1989-2005).

24 In 1890, a book appeared with the title of Might is Right, with the author listed as Ragnar Redbeard, a pseudonym. The book argues a social Darwinist position, that is only the strongest will survive. Usually used as a rationale to justify the elimination of a social safety net, Rowan is turning the argument around to say that the IWW, as rugged proletarians, will outlast government repression.

Chapter Seven: Frank Little

1 Little was signing up copper miners as he traveled around Arizona. These three had previously joined the IWW, but as members of other industrial union affiliates. Little, therefore, had to transfer them into the Metal Mine Workers' Industrial Union #800. Little was providing Perry with their previous card numbers and the date they joined the IWW and paid their initiation fee.

2 Prospecting for gold, or other valuable minerals, would seem to be an odd fantasy for a revolutionary socialist, but Frank Little was not the only miner turned Wobbly who still had the dream of striking it rich. In 1915, Vincent St. John left the post of general secretary-treasurer to prospect in New Mexico. He never hit pay dirt and died in poverty.

3 J.L. Donnelly was the president of the Arizona Federation of Labor, and a vehement opponent of the IWW and its drive to organize Arizona's copper miners.

4 IWW staff, whether field organizers or headquarters staff, received salaries comparable to the unskilled and semi-skilled workers they represented. Furthermore, there was a narrow differential in the pay received by the top officers and those in the field. Oates was receiving $18 a week, while Big Bill Haywood, as general secretary-treasurer, received $25 a week. This was a good plan, one that was consistent with the anti-hierarchical, egalitarian vision of the IWW.

In general, the concept worked well, but it needed to be modified in organizing Arizona's copper miners. Retail prices were high in isolated copper mining towns. Furthermore, copper miners were relatively well-paid for work that was dangerous and arduous. Most Arizona copper miners in 1917 were receiving $5.50 for an eight hour shift. With a six day work week standard, miners were earning $32.50 a week.

The IWW, therefore, found it hard to retain organizers in Arizona, so Perry opted to unofficially raise Joe Oates' pay to $25 a week. This still meant that Oates was getting paid significantly less than he would have received had he returned to the mines.

5 IWW members referred to the union as the General Organization. The union's overall decision making structure, as led by the General Executive Board and the General Secretary-Treasurer, was referred to as the General Office, or G.O.

6 *Solidarity* was the primary English language newspaper published by the IWW. Its editor, Ralph Chaplin, worked in the Chicago headquarters. *El Rebelde* was the Spanish language newspaper published by the IWW.

7 On June 17, 1917, a meeting of delegates from mining districts around Arizona had met to formulate a set of demands. The delegates decided to wait until the end of summer to present these demands to the mining companies. This would have allowed the Metal Mine Workers' Union to consolidate its organization throughout the state before entering into a confrontation. The Bisbee branch initiated a strike on June 27, 1917, well in advance of the date set by the previous state-wide meeting.

8 Briefs and Arguments for Plaintiffs and Defendants, Appeal to U.S. Circuit Court of Appeals, Haywood et al. v. USA, p. 544, Carton 2, Austin Lewis Papers, Special Collection, Bancroft Library, University of California, Berkeley, California.

9 Briefs and Arguments for Plaintiffs and Defendants, Appeal to U.S. Circuit Court of Appeals, Haywood et al. v. USA, p. 544, Carton 2, Austin Lewis Papers, Special Collection, Bancroft Library, University of California, Berkeley, California.

10 Briefs and Arguments for Plaintiffs and Defendants, Appeal to U.S. Circuit Court of Appeals, Haywood et al. v. USA, p. 545, Carton 2, Austin Lewis Papers, Special Collection, Bancroft Library, University of California, Berkeley, California.

11 A long, heavy sledgehammer used by miners.

12 Lena Perry, Grover Perry's wife, suffered a broken bone in a leg as a result of the same accident in which Frank Little incurred a broken bone in his right ankle that left him on crutches to the end of his life. Lena Perry was sent to the hospital to recover from her injury. The accident took place on June 20, 1917, on the road from Bisbee to Globe, Arizona, when their car went over a cliff. Grover Perry, *IWW Trial Transcript*, p. 10390.

13 This and the following footnote appeared in the original *Solidarity* article: Frank Little was arrested for reading the Declaration of Independence on the streets of Spokane. The cop said it was un-American. (Ed. note: Little was arrested during the Spokane, Washington, free speech fight in 1909.)

14 Governor Bell of Colorado said, "To Hell with the Constitution. We'll given them Post Mortems." This occurred at the time of the famous Cripple Creek strike in 1892. Some of the strikers and their friends complained that the treatment they received was unconstitutional. Up to the present, Bell has NOT been tried for treason or investigated in any way. (Ed. note: John Calhoun Bell was a U.S. federal district judge during the Cripple Creek strike. He was elected to the U.S. House of Representatives in November 1892 and served five terms.)

15 A placard was attached to Little's corpse when his body was left dangling from a railroad trestle. On the placard were written the numbers 3-7-77. This was a code used by vigilantes in Montana, and in other Western states as well. No one is certain as to the meaning of this set of numbers, but one plausible explanation is that they set the dimensions of a grave.

In addition to the numbers, several initials were written on the placard. These seemed to refer to several leading members of the Butte Metal Mine Workers' Union. The threat of additional killings was never carried through. Shortly after Little's murder, federal troops were stationed in Butte, so state repression replaced vigilante violence.

16 Jeannette Rankin was the sole member of the U.S. House of Representatives from Montana. She had opposed the U.S. entry into the war, but she later gave her support to the war effort. Rankin tried to stay neutral during the strike in Butte, although she did strongly condemn the murder of Frank Little.

Chapter Eight: Opposing the War

1 In addition to Haywood and Little, the resolution presented to the IWW Convention was signed by Francis Miller, a member of the General Executive Board, and W.E. Mattingly. Briefs and Arguments for Plaintiffs and Defendants, Appeal to U.S. Circuit Court of Appeals, Haywood et al. v. USA, p. 544, Carton 2, Austin Lewis Papers, Special Collection, Bancroft Library, University of California, Berkeley, California.

2 Briefs and Arguments for Plaintiffs and Defendants, Appeal to U.S. Circuit Court of Appeals, Haywood et al. v. USA, p. 546, Carton 2, Austin Lewis Papers, Special Collection, Bancroft Library, University of California, Berkeley, California.

3 Editorials appearing in *Solidarity* were written ten days to two weeks prior to the date of publication. Thus, this editorial, written by Ralph Chaplin, was drafted during the last week of March, 1917. At that point, the United States was preparing for war, although Congress did not officially declare war on Germany until April 6, 1917.

4 The Merchants and Manufacturers Association was formed in Los Angeles and spread through the West. It was committed to defeating every effort to organize unions, and pushed to keep towns 'open shop'.

5 In a letter dated April 24, 1917, (*IWW Transcript*, p. 13203), Ratti informed Sheridan: The flag was put up by the militia, having given orders to everyone in town to make us keep the one they put up.

6 Whitefish and Fortine are small logging communities in northwestern Montana, close to the Idaho border. St. Maries is a small logging community in northern Idaho.

7 Bisbee Collection, Special Collections, University of Arizona, Tucson, Arizona.

8 Briefs and Arguments for Plaintiffs and Defendants, Appeal to U.S. Circuit Court of Appeals, Haywood et al. v. USA, p. 542, Carton 2, Austin Lewis Papers, Special Collection, Bancroft Library, University of California, Berkeley, California.

9 Briefs and Arguments for Plaintiffs and Defendants, Appeal to U.S. Circuit Court of Appeals, Haywood et al. v. USA, p. 543, Carton 2, Austin Lewis Papers, Special Collection, Bancroft Library, University of California, Berkeley, California.

10 Box 1, Bisbee Collection, Special Collections, University of Arizona, Tucson, Arizona.

11 Little correctly describes the IWW's policy prior to U.S. entry into World war I in April 1917. The few Wobblies who volunteered to fight for the Allies by joining the Canadian Army were dropped from membership. Once the

United States joined the war, this policy was reversed. Those IWW members drafted into the U.S. military were not expelled, and, indeed, were welcomed back into the union after the war ended.

Chapter Nine: Conscription

1 Eastman was one of the defendants in the mass trial of Wobblies held in Wichita Kansas. He was found guilty and received a sentence of seven and a half years. Eastman evaded arrest for two years by going underground. He was captured and served his sentence at Leavenworth Federal Penitentiary from June 1919 to July 1922.

2 Briefs and Arguments for Plaintiffs and Defendants, Appeal to U.S. Circuit Court of Appeals, Haywood et al. v. USA, p. 545, Carton 2, Austin Lewis Papers, Special Collection, Bancroft Library, University of California, Berkeley, California.

3 The motion from the Kansas branch did not receive a response from Haywood at general headquarters, and was not considered by the General Executive Board.

4 J.P. Morgan and Co. was the most powerful firm of investment brokers in the United States. The British government relied on the firm to sell the bonds it issued to fund the war, and to act as its purchasing agent in the period prior to the U.S. decision to enter the war in April 1917.

Many opponents of the war believed that Woodrow Wilson was acting at the behest J.P. Morgan and Co. in pushing the United States into the war as an ally of the British government. Furthermore, they were convinced he had acted to prevent a German victory that would have rendered it impossible for the British to repay their vast debt, thereby causing the firm a considerable loss. This argument simplified a complex issue, but there is no doubt that the senior partners of J.P. Morgan wielded great power, and that they used this power to promote British interests.

5 Hardy was acting as a delegate, that is recruiting new members and collecting dues from current members, for both the Lumber Workers' Industrial Union #500 and the Construction Workers' Industrial Union #573.

6 Kalispell is a town in northwestern Montana. Whitefish is a small logging community in northwestern Montana, seventeen miles from Kalispell.

7 Rowan is evading the issue. The AFL had issued a statement of uncritical support for the war effort in March 1917. Gompers and the top AFL leaders placed enormous pressure on affiliated unions to adopt a similar position. The IWW could not wait for the AFL to reverse its position; it needed to act.

8 In the lingo of the IWW, a scissorbill was a worker who cooperated with the boss, in contrast to a class-conscious, militant Wobbly.

9 Irish immigrants had recently established the Pearse-Connolly club as a radical alternative to the more mainstream Irish clubs that had previously been established in Butte. Both Patrick (Padraig) Pearse and James Connolly were leaders of the Easter Uprising in Dublin in the spring of 1916, and both were executed by the British. Pearse was a nationalist with rather conservative politics, but Connolly was a revolutionary socialist who had worked with the IWW during his stay in the United States from the union's formation in 1905 until his departure for Ireland in 1910. Naming the club after Connolly was a clear signal to the Irish community in Butte that this was an organization for radicals.

10 Prejudice against immigrants from China was widespread throughout the West. This sentence is an unfortunate concession to popular prejudice in an otherwise excellent leaflet.

11 The Metal Mine Workers' Industrial Union Local 490 had been chartered by the IWW's General Executive Board in February 1916 to organize iron ore miners in upper Minnesota and the Upper Peninsula of Michigan.

12 Virginia is a mining town in northern Minnesota. Jacobson was a long-time resident of Virginia. He had worked as an iron ore miner before becoming secretary of MMWIU #490.

13 Indictment, United States of America v. William D. Haywood et al. (Chicago: Industrial Workers of the World, 1917), in Box 6, Industrial Workers of the World Papers, Catherwood Library, Cornell University, Ithaca, New York.

14 Harry Green wrote to Don Sheridan under the misunderstanding that Sheridan was still branch secretary of the Agricultural Workers' Industrial Union branch in Spokane. Sheridan had acted as interim secretary of the newly founded Lumber Workers' Industrial Union #500 from March 1917 to May 1917, when James Rowan, who had been elected secretary of the union, arrived in Spokane after traveling around the region organizing timber camps. Rowan then assumed the duties of the branch secretary for the Spokane region of the Agricultural Workers' Industrial Union #400 as well. He, therefore, responded to Green's letter.

Chapter Ten: Confronting Repression

1 Sheridan was acting as the interim secretary of the newly formed Lumber Workers' Industrial Union #500. This union had emerged from an organizing drive initiated by the Agricultural Workers' Industrial Union #400. This led to a confusion as to who would pay for the dues cards and union literature held at the Spokane headquarters of the Lumber Workers' Union. Haywood is trying to sort this out in this letter.

2 La Grande is a town in northeastern Oregon. Pasco is located in southeastern Washington. North Yakima, renamed Yakima in 1918, is a city in south central Washington. Ellensburg is a town in central Washington.

3 In June 1917, Governor William D. Stephens of California began urging the governors of the other Western states to coordinate their efforts to suppress the IWW. The meeting of Idaho's Governor Moses Alexander and Governor Ernest Lister of Washington was one of a series of discussions held in preparation for a larger conference of seven Western governors convened in August 1917 that adopted a coordinated plan developed in accordance with guidelines approved by the President.

4 Couer D'Alene is a city in northern Idaho.

5 Microfilm, Reel 11, Volume 86, American Civil Liberties Union Records (Glen Rock, NJ: Microfilming Corporation of America, 1976).

6 Senator Charles Thomas was a progressive Democrat. He served in the Senate from 1913 to 1921, when he was denied the nomination of the Democratic Party.

7 Starting in September 1917, dozens of IWW activists were imprisoned after union halls were raided around California. They were held until February 1918, when forty-six were indicted for allegedly violating the Espionage Act. All but three of them decided it would be a waste of money to hire an attorney, so they refused to participate in the trial. All of the defendants were convicted and twenty-six were sentenced to a ten-year prison term.

8 Most of the Kansas IWW defendants were arrested in the course of a raid on a union hall in November 1917. They were held on high bail in a barbaric prison until their trial in December 1918. Twenty-six of the defendants were convicted of violating the Espionage Act and received lengthy prison sentences that were served at Leavenworth Federal Penitentiary.

Index

Agricultural Workers' Industrial Union, #400 (IWW): and centralization, 8; and contract with Nonpartisan League, 14-17; organizes lumberjacks, 100

Agricultural Workers Organization (IWW), 28, 37, 100, 160

American Federation of Labor (AFL), 9, 19, 40, 73, 156

Anaconda Copper Mining Corporation, 76, 138

Bell, John Calhoun, 240n14

Bisbee, Montana, Strike (1917): aftermath, 97-99; begins, 80-83; demands of miners, 83-84; deportation, 91-96; shuts down mines, 86-87; and six-hour day, 88-90; spreads to other mines, 89-90;

Bobba, R.J., 98-99

Brazier, Richard: background of, 55, 107-108; and Joe Hill's execution, 57; 232n4; and lumberjack strike, 107-108; opposes conscription, 180-83; and sabotage, 38; and violence, 56

Brew, James, 93, 236n24

Brown, Roy, 126, 163, 238n22

Bureau of Investigation, 1-2, 197

Butte, Montana, strike (1917), 138

Cady, Frank, 43-45

California Commission of Immigration and Housing, 232n13-14

Calumet and Arizona Mine, 235n9

Campbell, Thomas Edward, 96

Chaplin, Ralph Hosea: on conscription, 194-95; as editor of *Solidarity*, 239n6; on World War I, 157-59, 241n3

Chicago conspiracy trial, 203, 210, 244n7

Clark, Stanley J., 86, 235n20

Cleary, William B., 81, 234n10

Commission on Industrial Relations, 232n12

Copper Queen Mine, 81, 86, 94, 234n10

criminal syndicalism law, 124, 189, 196, 200-201, 232n16, 238n21

Donnelly, J.L., 132, 239n3

Durst brothers' ranch, 24, 28

Eastman, Phineas, 242n1

Edwards, Forrest, 61-64

Embree, Adolphus Stewart, 80-84, 89, 236n25

Emergency Program (1924), 223

Espionage Act (1917), 38, 122, 126, 171, 194, 197

Ettor, Joseph, 27, 184, 231n5

Fanning, Raymond, 159-60

Farrar, Ross C., 66

Flynn, Elizabeth Gurley, 30-31, 33, 51, 201, 232n2

Folsom, C.J., 10, 229n5

Folsom Penitentiary, California, 26, 28

Ford, Richard (Blackie), 25-34, 57, 68

General Defense Committee, IWW, 208

General Executive Board, (IWW): and centralization, 8; and contract with Nonpartisan League, 15; copes with government repression, 203-205; and Frank Little's injuries, 131-33; and formation of Lumber Workers' Industrial Union, 101; and sabotage, 38-39; and war, 154, 167

George, Harrison, 159

Globe-Miami, Arizona, Strike, (1917), 81, 84, 86-90, 97-98, 134, 136

Green, Harry, 190-94

Hall, William Covington, 13, 230n8

Hardy, William, 175-76

Haymarket Square bomb, 229n2-3

Haywood, William Dudley: background of, 55; and Bisbee strike,

97; and conscription, 184-85; and Chicago conspiracy trial, 228n4, 233n5; and the Commission on Industrial relations, 231n12; and criminal syndicalism, 200-201; as general secretary-treasurer, 239n4; and Joe Hill, 57; on Little's injuries, 132; and private detectives, 198-99; and Schmidt case, 70; and the Socialist Party, 229n6; trial for murder, 231n4; on war, 153, 156, 165-67; and violence among migrant workers, 59-60; and Wheatland strike, 31, 35-36
Hill, Joe (Joel Emmanuel Hagglund): arrest of, 47; cremation of, 234n8; execution of, 51-57, 234n6; and women in the IWW, 49-50
Hutchins, Walter S., 21-24
Industrial Worker, 13, 185, 230n8
Jacobson, Charles, 97, 188-90
Johnson, Hiram Warren, 30, 32, 37, 230n8, 231n15
Justice, 43
Kansas trial (1919), 211, 245n8
Kimball, A.D., 82, 85, 234n11
Knights, Charles, 109-113
Lambert, Charles L., 29-36, 38, 184, 205
Law, Jack A., 12, 66, 68-71
Leavenworth, Kansas, Federal Penitentiary, 1, 208, 210
Little, Emma B., 144-45
Little, Frank H: assassination of 143-50; background of, 129; and Bisbee strike, 137; in Butte, 139, 142-43; injuries, 131-32, 134-36; opposes war, 140-42, 154, 165-69; organizing in Arizona, 238n1; and six-hour day, 77-80
Lloyd, Harold, 161-62
Loyalty League, 98-99
Ludlow, Colorado, confrontation, 232n1
lumberjack strike (1917): begins, 101-103; called off, 125-27; demands of strikers, 106-109; spreads, 104-105; suppression of, 116-120
Lumber Workers' Industrial Union #500 (IWW): 101, 109, 111-13, 172-73
MacKinnon, Charles, 89
Mahler, Herbert, 161-62, 205
McDonald, J.A., 85
McNutt, Maxwell, 231n9
Metal Mine Workers' Industrial Union #490, 242n9
Metal Mine Workers' Industrial Union #800, (IWW), 8, 73-74, 78, 80, 83, 87-89
Miller, Francis D., 38, 133, 205
Moore, Frederick H., 97
Morgan, J.P. and Co., 75, 242n4
Moyer, Charles H: and Arizona locals, 75, 234n4; background of, 233n3; IWW hatred of, 76-77; as president of the Western Federation of Miners, 234n3; trial for murder, 231n4
Nef, Walter T., 106-107, 160-61, 205
Nonpartisan League, 8, 14-15
Oates, Joseph, 88-89, 131-32, 205, fn 3, Litt
People's Councils of America for Democracy and the Terms of Peace, 155, 169
Pearse-Connolly club, 243n9
Perry, Grover H.: background of, 74; and the Chicago conspiracy trial, 233n2; and Little's injuries, 132; and six-hour day, 88-90
Perry, Lena, 137, 143, 241n12
Phelps Dodge Corporation fn 9 bis
Pinkerton Detective Agency, 199
Rankin, Jeannette Pickering, 149, 240n16
Ratti, Joseph J., 104-105, 119, 162-64, 177-78, 241n5
Redhead, Ragnar (pseud.), 127, 238n24

Rowan, James H.: assessment of lumberjack strike, 127-28; background, 101; calls general strike, 102, 116; on conscription, 176, 178-79; on contracts, 114; detained by military, 238n18; on government repression, 117-20, 206-207; on sabotage, 113; on violence, 120-21

sabotage: and black cat, 237n8; IWW opposes, 38-39; types of, 18-21; and Wheatland strike, 25-37; and work to rule, 21-24

Sacramento Bee, 34-35

Sacramento conspiracy trial (1919), 210, 245n7

St. John, Vincent: background of, 9; and centralization, 9-13, 229n4; and private detectives, 198-99; as prospector, 239n2; and violence, 44-47; on Wheatland strike, 32-33

Scharrenberg, Paul, 231n13

Schmidt, James, 66-72

Shattuck, Lemuel Coover, 81

Shattuck Mine, 82, 235n9

Sherman, Gerald Fitzgerald, 81, 234n12

Sheridan, Donald: calls off lumberjacks strike, 123-26; and Chicago conspiracy trial, 237n17; and start of lumberjacks strike, 103-104; as secretary of the Lumber Workers' Industrial Union, 243n1; on war, 164

Shingle Weavers' Union, (AFL), 9-11

six-hour day, 77-80, 88-90, 236n22

1. *Solidarity,* 157, 185

Speculator Mine Fire (1917), 74, 83, 138

Speed, George, 30, 230n10

Spry, William, 232n3

Stephens, William Dennison, 244n3

Steunenberg, 56, 231n4

Suhr, Herman D., 25-34, 68

Thompson, James Patrick, 9-10, 86, 137

Townley, Arthur Charles, 15

Voice of the People, 13

Ward, D.B., 114-15

Webb, Benjamin, 81, 84

Western Federation of Miners (WFM): background of, 73; becomes International Union of Mine, Mill and Smelter Workers, 234n1; IWW hatred of, 76-77

Wheatland, California, strike: 24-37

Wheeler, Harry Cornwall, 82, 235n16

Wiertola, William, 38, 205

Williams, Benjamin H., 57, 60

About the Author

ERIC THOMAS CHESTER has been a socialist activist for fifty years, beginning in the 1960s with the civil rights movement and Students for a Democratic Society. In 1996, he stood as the Socialist Party's vice-presidential candidate. He is currently a member of the Industrial Workers of the World and the Republican Communist Network of Scotland. After graduating from the University of Michigan, he taught economics at the University of Massachusetts-Boston. His published works include *Covert Network* (1995), an investigation of the International Rescue Committee, and *Rag-Tags, Scum, Riff-Raff and Commies* (2001), a history of the U.S. intervention in the Dominican Republic in 1965. He recently finished a new work, *The Wobblies in Their Heyday: The Rise and Destruction of The Industrial Workers of the World During the World War I Era* (2014, Levellers Press paperback, 2016).